COMMON SENSE MANAGEMENT

Roger Fulton

COMMON SENSE MANAGEMENT

Quick Wisdom *for* Good Managers

TEN SPEED PRESS
Berkeley | Toronto

Ten Speed Press
PO Box 7123
Berkeley, California 94707
www.tenspeed.com

Distributed in Australia by Simon and Schuster Australia, in Canada by Ten Speed Press Canada, in New Zealand by Southern Publishers Group, in South Africa by Real Books, and in the United Kingdom and Europe by Publishers Group UK.

Cover and text design by Tracy White

Portions of this book were previously published in *Common Sense Supervision* (Ten Speed Press, 1988) and *Common Sense Leadership* (Ten Speed Press, 1995)

Library of Congress Cataloging-in-Publication Data
Fulton, Roger.
  Common sense management : quick wisdom for good managers / Roger Fulton.
    p. cm.
  Summary: "A motivational book for supervisors and managers, featuring
practical advice on getting the most from employees"—Provided by publisher.
    ISBN 978-1-58008-983-8
1. Supervision of employees. 2. Management. I. Title.
  HF5549.12.F85 2009
  658.3'02—dc22
                          2008043587

Printed in the United States of America on recycled paper (30% PCW)

First printing, 2009
1 2 3 4 5 6 7 8 9 10 — 13 12 11 10 09

CONTENTS

1   INTRODUCTION

PART ONE: SUPERVISION

6   *Chapter One* Your Introduction to Supervision

8   *Chapter Two* You and Your Organization

16   *Chapter Three* You as a Supervisor

26   *Chapter Four* Winning Respect

37   *Chapter Five* Winning Confidence

44   *Chapter Six* What the Best Supervisors Do

52   *Chapter Seven* Quick Wisdom: Supervision

PART TWO: MANAGEMENT

56   *Chapter Eight* Your Introduction to Management

58   *Chapter Nine* Preventing and Handling Problems

67   *Chapter Ten* Being a Good Administrator

74   *Chapter Eleven* Winning Loyalty

82   *Chapter Twelve* What the Best Managers Do

92   *Chapter Thirteen* Quick Wisdom: Management

PART THREE: LEADERSHIP

96 *Chapter Fourteen* Your Introduction to Leadership

100 *Chapter Fifteen* Leaders Prepare By . . .

108 *Chapter Sixteen* Leaders Are . . .

121 *Chapter Seventeen* Leaders Understand . . .

136 *Chapter Eighteen* Leaders Avoid . . .

152 *Chapter Nineteen* Leaders Lead By . . .

168 *Chapter Twenty* Quick Wisdom: Leadership

170 **EPILOGUE**

INTRODUCTION

Welcome!

Thank you for selecting this book. I've designed it with your future success in mind.

In it, you will find very practical tips on how to be a successful supervisor and manager. And once you master those two categories, you'll find tips on how to be a successful leader as well.

But let's not get too far ahead of ourselves. There are some basic ideas and concepts you will need to embrace before we get started.

This Is the Real World

This book is about your success in the real business world and your involvement in it. No matter what industry you have chosen, profit/nonprofit, manufacturing, or service, this world is real.

You are no longer in that safe school environment. In the business world, you are judged on your ability to get things done. Your successes and your failures are your grading system and the stakes are high. Success leads to promotions and higher pay and benefits. Failure sends you to the unemployment line, and you must start all over again with one strike against you.

So if you value driving a good car, living in a nice place, and having the respect of all who work with you, you will want to pay attention to the ideas, tips, and rules presented in this book.

Rules

In general, if you want to be successful in your chosen industry, then you must follow the general rules of that industry. In most cases, those rules are common sense.

If you work around gasoline, then don't smoke. If you work near deep water, you might want to invest in swimming lessons and a life jacket. If you work with people, you might want to learn how to get along with them.

In this book, I'll give you rules, tips, and guidelines for being a successful supervisor, manager, and leader in any industry. It's all designed so that you don't accidentally blow yourself up, you don't drown in your efforts to succeed, and you learn how to get along with people.

People

Business is about people. They come in the form of customers, suppliers, coworkers, subordinates, and bosses. And how you interact with all of those people will determine your own success.

Keep in mind that those people, at all levels, are the key to the success of any business. Without people, there is no business, and if there is no business, there is no work for you as a result.

Throughout this book, please remember that people are the key to your success or failure as a supervisor, manager, or leader.

Moving Forward

Take a deep breath, contemplate your future briefly, and read on to get started on the road to the success of your own career.

> The future belongs to those who dare.
> *Anonymous*

Joining the Management Team

Once you have proven yourself as a good and dedicated employee, you can expect to be promoted to a supervisory position. There you will not only be responsible for your own performance but also for the performance of other employees.

That promotion will make you a part of the management team. This team consists of you, your boss, your boss's boss, and so on, up the organizational ladder. And you will all have one major goal: to get the job done correctly and on time, whatever that job is in your organization.

In the following paragraphs, we will look at what each stage means and how you fit into the various categories of management responsibilities. The explanations relate directly to the three parts of this book.

Supervision: Overseeing the work of other people. That means making sure that they do their work and meet the goals and deadlines as expected.

Management: Bringing people and things together to be sure that the job gets done on time. It requires getting people, equipment, and parts to the right place at the right time so it all comes together as a final and complete package.

Leadership: Having the vision to look ahead and know where you and your unit are headed in the future and getting everyone on board to help you all get there. (Hint: to be a successful leader, you must also be a successful supervisor and manager.)

Let's review the job skills required of supervisors, managers, and leaders and how they interact. The supervisor oversees the work of people. The manager brings people and things together. And the leader has the vision to put it all together and take the group where it needs to go. These three categories all interact and build on one another, regardless of the job title.

Leaders can't get anything done without people—and that means motivated people with excellent supervision and management skills. And you can reverse it and say that supervisors and managers can't get anything done unless they have leaders to show them the way and give them the necessary equipment and resources to get the job done.

So let's make it clear that you will need to learn all of the skills presented in this book to be a good supervisor, a good manager, and a good leader. Put them all together and you will succeed within your organization. It's all very simple once you know the rules to follow and the problems to avoid. And this book will help you to do just that.

Best wishes for a long and successful career in your chosen industry, no matter how high up the ladder you choose to go.

—Roger Fulton

PART ONE

SUPERVISION
YOUR FUTURE
BEGINS
RIGHT HERE

CHAPTER 1

YOUR INTRODUCTION TO SUPERVISION

Once you have proven yourself as a reliable, dependable, and very capable worker, your employer will think that you are an excellent role model for others in the organization. Then he will want to promote you from basic worker to overseeing the work of some small group of other workers. In essence, you will become a supervisor of others and their work. That small promotion will come with a pay raise and added responsibilities.

Supervising the work activities of other people can be a rewarding and satisfying experience. It can give you the opportunity to coordinate the activities of several people, or several groups of people, and to ultimately see the fruits of their efforts turn into a fully developed final product—one that no single person could produce alone.

Don't Panic

Dozens of ideas, proven concepts, and solutions are presented on the following pages. They are presented in a practical, concise, commonsense form so that you can start using them tomorrow to be the best supervisor that you can be. It should be noted, however, that this section does not tell you how to handle every situation. That would be impossible since every situation, every employee, and every supervisor is different.

The key to successful supervision is your ability to handle the unique and unusual situations that will confront you throughout your career. The material contained in this book will give you guidelines for success, but it is you, and you alone, who must use this wisdom and your own common sense when handling each new and challenging situation.

Can You Be a Successful Supervisor?

The answer to that question is that most people can succeed as a supervisor. But just as with success in anything, it will require knowledge, training, experience, and a great deal of effort on your part. Other people can help you, but it is you who must put forth the effort to succeed.

In addition to having the common sense to pick up this book, you already have completed several steps toward your success:

1. Your superiors already have faith in your abilities to be a supervisor since they have given you that title.

2. You probably already have a great deal of knowledge and experience in your own industry that can give you insight into future problems and solutions.

3. You already have a positive attitude toward your work and your company since you have put forth the effort to be successful in your career thus far.

Given these assets, it should not be difficult for you to build on them and to reach true success as a supervisor of others.

> Success usually comes to those who are too busy to be looking for it.
> *Henry David Thoreau*

CHAPTER 2

YOU AND YOUR ORGANIZATION

> No man is an island, entire of itself; every man is
> a piece of the continent, a part of the main . . .
>
> *John Donne*

Your Role as a Supervisor

As a supervisor, you will be responsible for the activities and performance of others, not just for your own performance. Your job is now less defined with more gray areas.

Your time will be at a premium. Initially you will feel that there are barely enough hours in the day to get everything done. You will tend to take the job home with you more—not just paperwork, but the problems of the day as well.

You must learn to be a buffer between your own supervisors and your employees. Both sides have their own goals, desires, and needs. Your job is to keep them both reasonably happy and satisfied while keeping yourself happy and satisfied as well.

Sound difficult? A little overwhelming? Relax. It's easier than you think, and it is well worth the effort.

> The executive exists to make sensible exceptions
> to general rules.
>
> *Elting E. Morison*

Executive Privileges

Even if you are not a true executive, the quality of your life has substantially increased by becoming a supervisor. People will have more respect for you since you have advanced in your job. Your paycheck will go up considerably. You will probably be getting better fringe benefits: more insurance, longer vacations. You will be treated much better by upper-level management. You'll have better access to the boss and you'll be able to assist in policy-making decisions.

Enjoy those benefits! You have earned them and you will continue to earn them every day.

> Each honest calling, each walk of life, has its own elite, its own aristocracy based upon excellence of performance.
>
> *James Bryant Conant*

Getting Along with the Boss

This is priority one! Your boss can make your life very difficult for you or very easy for you. Here are a few rules to follow:

1. Don't take up too much of her time; just enough to get the information and guidance you need.

2. Don't be afraid of the boss. The boss needs you as much as you need the boss. Remember that her job is to get things done through people—and you are one of those people.

3. Keep in mind that all bosses are people and all people have quirks. Therefore, all bosses have quirks. Learn them and heed them. It'll be to your advantage.

4. Never embarrass the boss, intentionally or accidentally.

If you can get along with the boss, you've gone a long way toward success as a supervisor.

> It has been well said that "he who has never learned to obey cannot be a good commander."
>
> *Aristotle*

The Informal Organization

This—the informal employee power structure—is the underground! It is made up of regular workers who are respected by other workers for their experience, their knowledge, or their connections. They control the pipeline for the informal rumors and information among the employees.

Handle this informal organization, or it will handle you. It can make you or break you, depending on what is said by you and about you.

How do you handle it? By being fair and up front with all of your employees, with specific attention to the informal leaders. Just treat them right in their jobs and let them know what's going on—informally, of course. Then they will spread the truth about you and the organization rather than circulating false rumors and innuendos.

If you're fair to all, you'll fare well.

> The first and great commandment is:
> Don't let them scare you.
>
> *Elmer Davis*

Morale

Morale can be affected positively or negatively by an incident that seems insignificant to you, but which may be very important to your employees. A happy crew will do more and better work than an unhappy crew.

Rumors and unfairness are the enemies of good morale. If there is unfair treatment of one employee, all the other employees will feel that they may be next in line for this unfair treatment. If you know what is going on in your department, you can straighten out misunderstandings or dispel false rumors before they adversely affect employee morale.

A high level of employee morale is your ultimate goal. Following the principles set out in future pages will assist you in achieving this goal.

Always keep in mind that subordinates of excellent leaders have excellent morale. Subordinates of poor leaders have poor morale.

> Abuse a man unjustly, and you will make friends for him.
>
> *Edgar Watson Howe*

Esprit de Corps

Esprit de corps means the employees' pride in their work and in the organization. Outside recognition for excellent performance, whether from the media, other organizations, professional associations, or your own organization will lead to excellent esprit de corps.

As a supervisor, you should seek out these types of awards for your people and strive for the excellence to obtain them. Let your people know you are seeking to obtain awards, not for you, but for them, because they deserve to be acknowledged.

In the everyday environment, encourage employees to do their collective best to perform as a team—the best team—in the business. They will feel better about themselves and work better for you and the organization.

> Destiny is not a matter of chance, it is a matter of choice; it is nothing to be waited for, it is a thing to be achieved.
>
> *William Jennings Bryan*

Internal Conflict

Stay in your own domain. You will have enough to do with your own job. Don't try to meddle in another department's affairs unless your failure to take action will adversely affect your department's performance.

Resolve interdepartmental conflicts with your equal in the other department. If you have given the other supervisor the opportunity to resolve it informally between the two of you, and have met with unreasonable resistance, then you are justified in advising your superior and having him assist in resolving the problem.

Carefully choose which battles you are willing to fight. Not all battles are worth the resulting bad feelings or long-term problems that will result, even if you win. However, some are. You get paid for your judgment. Use it wisely.

Strive mightily, but eat and drink as friends.

William Shakespeare

Competition from Peers

This is related to what you just read. The organizational structure is a pyramid and it gets narrow at the top. When several good people (you and your peers) vie for the next highest level in the pyramid, there can be very stiff competition.

Protect yourself at all times. Don't get pushed around, but don't look for trouble either.

In the heat of the competition, don't be a backstabber or an end-runner. Both of these will cost you dearly in the end.

Your best overall strategy in the competition is to be loyal, mind your own business, and do your job to the best of your ability. You'll come out a true winner in the long haul.

> I studied the lives of great men and famous women, and I found that the men and women who got to the top were those who did the jobs they had in hand, with everything they had of energy and enthusiasm and hard work.
>
> *Harry S. Truman*

This is the end of chapter two. See how easy it was to start learning your new role?

Now that you have a good idea about the forces within your organization and their relationship to you, let's turn to what you should be doing as a first-rate supervisor.

> The secret of joy in your work is contained in one word—excellence. To know how to do something well is to enjoy it.
>
> *Pearl Buck*

CHAPTER 3

YOU AS A SUPERVISOR

> A competent leader can get efficient service from poor troops; while on the contrary, an incapable leader can demoralize the best troops.
>
> *General John J. Pershing*

Set the Example

Your conduct, appearance, attitude, and work habits will set the tone for your employees' conduct, appearance, attitude, and work habits. In short, be a model employee and others will pattern themselves after you.

Show up on time or, preferably, early. Dress appropriately for your business. Don't do personal business on company time. Don't spend an hour reading the newspaper, drinking coffee, or goofing off. Get right to your job.

Gossip, complaining, and laziness have no place in a supervisor's office.

> Always do right. This will gratify some people, and astonish the rest.
>
> *Mark Twain*

Be Technically Proficient

Know your job. You probably have a good technical background in your industry or you would not have been chosen to be a supervisor. However, when it comes to being a supervisor, the technical problems are usually easy. It's the people problems that can cause the greatest difficulty.

You already have the right idea about improving your supervisory skills because you are reading this book. However, this is only a guide. It does not contain everything you will ever need to know about your whole job.

Attend technical seminars to keep all of your technical skills up to date in this rapidly changing technological age. Try to attend management workshops and seminars to hone your people skills as well. A progressive organization will welcome your initiative and will usually pay the expenses for both technical and personnel management educational programs.

How can you go wrong?

> Anyone who stops learning is old, whether at twenty or eighty. Anyone who keeps learning stays young.
>
> *Henry Ford*

Make a Decision!

The worst decision is no decision.

In order for a decision to be worthwhile, it must be sound and made in a timely fashion.

The people above you have faith in your ability to make decisions or they would not have made you a supervisor. However, as we all know, not all decisions are good decisions. But if decisions are based on the following process, they should never be bad decisions:

1. Gather all the facts you need to understand the situation.

2. Analyze the facts and review them objectively.

3. Formulate possible strategies and consider the consequences of each.

4. Choose the best strategy and make a plan to implement it.

Some decisions are made in seconds, some in days, and some in months. However, they all are made the same way following these simple guidelines.

If you can't make a decision, or consistently make the wrong one, then being a supervisor is not for you and you should choose another career path.

> Nothing is more difficult, and therefore more precious, than to be able to decide.
>
> *Napoleon Bonaparte*

Take Responsibility for Your Actions

This means taking responsibility whether you are right or wrong. Don't try to pass the buck; it stops at your desk.

If you made a decision based on the decision process outlined earlier, then be sure to stand by that decision and cite the reasons why you made that decision.

If your supervisor says your decision was wrong and must be changed, then it is no longer your decision. It is her decision and she must take the responsibility for it.

Chances are that you will seldom be called wrong by a good supervisor. Usually she will let your decision stand. If it wasn't the best alternative, then she will give you a chance to modify your decision, but he won't necessarily change it.

Keep in mind that your boss understands the decision-making process and has to rely on you in the future. She understands that you will not be perfect every time. If you were, she couldn't afford you.

One last point on this: Seldom will success or failure depend on one simple decision. If you are right (or nearly right) the majority of the time in decision making, you will be considered successful.

> We do our best that we know how at the
> moment, and if it doesn't turn out, we modify it.
> *Franklin D. Roosevelt*

Know Yourself

There is not one among us who is perfect in every way and in every situation. However, by knowing your own strengths and weaknesses, you can maximize your strengths and minimize your weaknesses.

Once you know and understand yourself, the business of knowing and understanding others will be much easier.

> When a man points a finger at someone else, he should remember that four of his fingers are pointing at himself.
>
> *Louis Nizer*

Maintain a Positive Attitude

Both your success and the success of your employees will depend on your attitude. If you have a positive attitude toward your work and the organization's goals, then your actions and words will convey that positive attitude to your employees. If you convey a negative attitude, then the employees will key in on your negativity.

If you are to maintain a healthy and productive atmosphere in the workplace, you must have a healthy and productive attitude toward your work and your organization.

> Man is what he believes.
>
> *Anton Chekhov*

Handle Personal Stress

Is being a supervisor stressful? Yes. Is that stress harmful to you? Not necessarily.

It's all in how you handle it. Be concerned and conscientious, but don't be a worrier.

The organization was here before you got here and will be here long after you are gone.

Do the best you can to maintain and improve the organization, but don't constantly worry about every little thing or you will destroy yourself and be of no value to anyone.

Accept those things that you cannot change, but change those things that you can.

> To accept whatever comes, regardless of the consequences, is to be unafraid.
>
> *John Cage*

Give Orders Properly

Many supervisors fail miserably in this area. Here are some simple guidelines.

In routine matters, "could you," "would you," "as soon as you get a chance," and the like are phrases you should use when asking someone to do something.

In emergency or high-priority situations, direct orders are appropriate: "do . . . ," "go . . . ," "handle this immediately . . . ," and so on.

Naturally a simple "please" followed by a "thank you" is nearly always appropriate.

> What you cannot enforce, do not command.
>
> *Sophocles*

Don't Expect Too Much

Ensure that the quantity and quality of the work you expect is set at a reasonable level.

If people are pushed beyond their limits for an extended period of time, they will burn out and productivity will decrease just when you need it most. By setting reasonable standards, you can be sure that you will still have employees who, on occasion, can and will work harder to meet an unexpected deadline.

> A good horse should be seldom spurred.
> *Thomas Fuller*

Maintain Your Sense of Humor

Maintaining your sense of humor will carry you through some of the most difficult times in your career. When things get really crazy at work, try to remember this little poem. It may be a little silly, but it always brings a smile to my face whenever I think about it.

> *When things go wrong as they sometimes will;*
> *and all your life seems all uphill;*
> *When your career is crumbling,*
> *and production is tumbling;*
> *Stop and reflect that despite your best;*
> *how funny you look in all that mess.*

Your failure to maintain your sense of humor could end your career quickly if you allow your frustration to build to the breaking point without relief.

> You grow up the day you have the first real laugh—at yourself.
> *Ethel Barrymore*

Stop here and reflect for a few minutes on these last few pages. Ask yourself these questions:

1. Are you a good example for your people to follow?
2. Are you as good as you can be?
3. Can you make a sound and timely decision based on the facts?
4. Do you care about your people?

If you answered yes to all of these questions, then you are well on your way to being a successful supervisor. Continue reading.

If you answered no to any of these questions, take a few more minutes, or longer, and make a commitment to improve in that weak area. Once committed, read on.

> Individual commitment to a group effort—that is what makes a team work, a company work, a society work, a civilization work.
>
> *Vince Lombardi*

CHAPTER 4

WINNING RESPECT

Few people can actually define respect. But we know whom we do respect and whom we don't respect. The following pages should help you to be a supervisor that your employees will respect.

> The leader must know, must know that he knows, and must be able to make it abundantly clear to those about him that he knows.
> *Clarence B. Randall*

Be Businesslike

If you want to be respected, always be a professional in every way. Look as if you know what you are doing. Here are a few specifics:

- Be put together, not rumpled or ruffled.
- Don't engage in horseplay or practical jokes.
- Don't use obscene or vulgar language.
- Rumors, sexism, racism, ethnic jokes, sarcasm, and gossip: none of these have any place in the workplace.

> Those who command themselves, command others.
> *Anonymous*

Maintain a Good Personal Appearance

Here are some more specifics:

- Be neat.
- Look disciplined.
- Keep your hair cut and well groomed.
- Wear appropriate business attire for your particular industry. (Some might say, dress for the job you want.)
- Always look like a professional and set the example.

> A man, in order to establish himself in the world, does everything he can to appear established there.
>
> *François La Rochefoucauld*

Maintain Discipline

Don't tolerate disrespect or laziness.

Be sure that your people know the rules, understand the quality and quantity of the work that is required, and maintain the standard of conduct you expect them to maintain.

Then enforce the rules with a fair and just hand, equally for all. Maintaining a high but not unreasonable level of discipline will save you many problems in the future. The ultimate compliment for a supervisor is to be known by his people as "firm but fair."

That is your goal.

> The superior man is firm in the right way, not merely firm.
>
> *Confucius*

Exhibit Personal Integrity

No kickbacks, no favors, no lies, no misleading.

If you engage in any of the above, it will come back to haunt you when you least expect it. Keep in mind that your employees observe you and your conduct every day. They know more of your business than you think they do.

If they are to have respect for you, your personal integrity must be above reproach.

> The measure of a man's real character is what he would do if he knew he never would be found out.
>
> *Thomas Macaulay*

Handle Friendships with Subordinates Carefully

Very carefully.

As a supervisor, you are in a different position than you were in your previous position.

Those people worth having as friends will understand the difference between on-duty and off-duty familiarity and will respect it. Those people not worthy as friends will try to use off-duty familiarity to gain an advantage when on duty.

One cardinal rule that you must never violate: romance has no place in the workplace.

> In a social order where one member is officially subordinate to another, the superior, if he is a gentleman, never thinks of it; and the subordinate, if he is a gentleman, never forgets it.
>
> *General John J. Pershing*

Take Personal Responsibility for Errors

You are the boss. If your subordinates perform well, then you have performed well.

If they do not perform well, then you have not performed well. Never try to place the blame on others.

You are the supervisor and you are ultimately responsible for everything your people do—good or bad. You cannot shirk this responsibility.

If a mistake occurs, correct the errors and take the steps necessary to ensure that it doesn't happen again. Then go on from there.

> To be nobly wrong is more manly than to be meanly right.
>
> *Thomas Paine*

Be Patient and Calm

Use self-control at all times. When things are not going well, it is up to you to find a sound, rational solution. You can only do that if you are thinking clearly and rationally.

If an emergency arises, others will look to you for guidance and an end to the problem situation.

If you are not in control of yourself, you become a part of the problem, not a part of the solution.

> In all good things, reason should prevail.
>
> *William Penn*

Be Consistent

Don't enforce the rules today and ignore them tomorrow. People are content in knowing what is expected from them, and they adjust to the rules even when the rules and the enforcement are strict. Therefore don't be erratic, or your employees will not know what is truly expected of them. Your inconsistency will translate into employee disciplinary problems and an uneasy feeling throughout your department.

Consistency is critical to your success as a supervisor.

> Nothing that isn't a real crime makes a man appear so contemptible and little in the eyes of the world as inconsistency.
>
> *Joseph Addison*

Expect Good Conduct

Don't tolerate dangerous horseplay or demeaning practical jokes. A little harmless fun is often good for morale, but be sure it's not overdone.

Under your guidance, employees will learn the limits and will conform their conduct to those limits.

Failure to maintain this standard can result in serious consequences for you, the employees, and your organization in the form of complaints, injuries and, eventually, lawsuits.

> In every real man, a child is hidden that wants to play.
>
> *Friedrich Nietzsche*

Expect Good Work

If a project isn't done right, tell the employee what is wrong with it, the right way to do it, and have them do it correctly.

If the work still isn't done correctly after that, keep returning it until it is done correctly.

Maintain your standards of excellence at all times. Your employees will learn what standard is expected of them and will perform to that standard accordingly. If you allow shoddy work, then shoddy work will become the standard of your department over time.

> The difference between failure and success is doing a thing nearly right and doing a thing exactly right.
>
> *Edward Simmons*

Acknowledge Good Work with Praise

Don't praise just to praise, but let your employees know you care and that you noticed their efforts. The thought that a person works for money alone has been disproved by innumerable researchers. The most satisfying reason for a person to work is that it makes that person feel worthwhile and that he is making a contribution to some larger effort.

Recognition of a worker's personal efforts will pay dividends a thousand times to you and to the organization.

> A pat on the back is only a few vertebrae removed from a kick in the pants, but is miles ahead in results.
>
> *V. Wilcox*

Praise in Public, Chastise in Private

This is a cardinal rule. Don't ever forget it.

Anything said in public, becomes public. There is no need to embarrass an employee in front of peers or other supervisors. If it is necessary to chastise an employee for poor work or conduct, do it in the privacy of your office.

However, if an employee has performed in an excellent manner, you can make that employee a proud individual by praising her efforts in the presence of coworkers.

> I have yet to find a man, however exalted his station, who did not do better work and put forth greater effort under a spirit of approval than under a spirit of criticism.
>
> *Charles Schwab*

Avoid Unnecessary Activity

Don't make work for your employees. If goals are set and employees work hard to finish early, don't ruin it by forcing them to do unnecessary extra work.

You can plan in advance for slow periods by arranging for vacation time or personal time off for employees during nonpeak periods to avoid having to keep employees "busy" during these times.

Also try to keep paperwork to a minimum. Very few people enjoy doing paperwork. If your employees view it as unnecessary or redundant, they will resent it even more.

> It is not enough to be industrious; so are the ants. What are you industrious about?
>
> *Henry David Thoreau*

Know What Is Going On

Don't sit in your office all day. You won't learn anything except what somebody wants you to know.

Practice MBWA: Management By Walking Around. Get out and talk to your people. They will tell you what is really happening, either directly or by dropping hints.

You can gauge morale, prevent potential problems, and develop an open dialogue with your employees by spending time with them.

In your travels, don't forget to talk to other supervisors as well as members of upper-level management. (They should be walking around as well.) That way you can get the big picture of what is happening in your organization so you might be able to anticipate future demands on your department.

> There is no knowledge, no light, no wisdom that you are in possession of, but what you have received from some source.
>
> *Brigham Young*

Be Impartial

Treat everyone equally. Don't play favorites, and set personal prejudices aside.

In some ways, you are like a judge in a court. You must resolve employee conflicts. You must balance production concerns and people concerns. You must balance labor concerns and management concerns.

In order to do this effectively and successfully, and with the support of all parties, you must be recognized as an impartial judge of the facts.

> Unless justice be done to others it will not be done to us.
>
> *Woodrow Wilson*

By now you have learned some guidelines for how to win the respect of your employees, your peers, and your bosses. Next it's time to learn the basics of how to win the confidence of those people, and how to be confident in your own abilities as you progress down your chosen career path.

> Respect commands itself and it can neither be given nor withheld when it is due.
>
> *Eldridge Cleaver*

WINNING CONFIDENCE

If your people don't have confidence in you and your abilities, then they will isolate you from their problems and ignore you when they need a solution. Ultimately you will have no idea, and no control over, what is going on in your department.

The following pages contain a few simple rules for gaining the confidence of your employees.

> Whether you believe you can do a thing or not, you are right.
>
> *Henry Ford*

Appear Confident

Look as if you know what you are doing (even when you have doubts).

The best way to appear confident is to have faith in yourself and your capabilities. The best way to have faith in your capabilities is to be knowledgeable, experienced, and able to systematically work through any problem in a calm and efficient manner.

> The world is governed more by appearances than by realities, so that it is fully as necessary to seem to know something as to know it.
>
> *Daniel Webster*

Be Available

You must make time for your people; they are your most valuable resource.

Communication is an art with many flaws. Even though you try to make things perfectly clear through oral and written orders, there are times when employees need a decision or the answer to a simple question to properly complete the task at hand. If you are not available for consultation, then the project may not continue in the proper direction. If it goes in the wrong direction, you have wasted a great deal of time, effort, and money, all for the want of a short consultation with you for clarification or guidance.

> Every great mistake has a halfway moment, a split second when it can be recalled and perhaps remedied.
>
> *Pearl S. Buck*

Encourage Free Speech

If your employees don't talk to you, they'll talk to each other and leave you in the dark.

If you know about a problem, you can handle it. If you don't know, then the problem can only get worse and you will have no control over it.

Many grievances are resolved just by bringing the issue to the attention of the boss, whether or not he can do anything about it.

Listen to new ideas; consider them on their merits and implement those that can benefit the employees, the department, or the organization.

> Words are the best medium of exchange of thoughts and ideas between people.
>
> *William Ross*

Keep Your People Informed

There are very few necessary secrets in most industries. Keeping your employees informed of what is going on in the organization eliminates unfounded rumors and lets them understand the bigger picture.

If you keep them accurately informed, they will learn to come to you for the facts—and will learn to trust you in the process.

> Nothing is so burdensome as a secret.
>
> *French Proverb*

Insist on Honesty

Don't tolerate lies or deceitful conduct. Investigate, research facts, and directly confront anyone who is deceitful or who openly lies to cover up a problem.

Word will quickly spread that you don't tolerate dishonesty among your employees. This type of up-front policy will benefit you in handling problem situations and will ultimately benefit the entire organization as well.

> Hateful to me as the Gates of Hades is that man who hides one thing in his heart and speaks another.
>
> *Homer*

Keep Promises

Or don't make them.

Promise to try, but don't promise what you cannot guarantee.

In the same vein, if you promise a subordinate that you will perform a certain task for her, then be sure to do it. And do it in a timely fashion. By doing so, she will learn to trust you and will learn to have confidence in you, your word, and your ability to get things done.

> Who breaks his faith, no faith is held with him.
>
> *Guillame de Salluste Du Bartas*

Give Credit for Ideas

It makes employees feel good and builds up morale to know that they had input into a decision or product.

If you steal their ideas and claim they are yours, it will be noticed.

Result? They'll never come up with new ideas again—at least not ones that you'll hear about.

> The most powerful factors in the world are clear ideas in the minds of energetic men of good will.
>
> *John Arthur Thomson*

Don't Criticize Superiors

Just as you have to make decisions in your position, your supervisors have to make their decisions. Even if you don't agree with a superior's decision, it is still your responsibility to implement that decision.

Criticizing your supervisors' decisions in front of your people serves no purpose. The fact that you were critical will get back to your supervisors and they will realize that you cannot be relied on to support them.

Your days will then be numbered in your organization.

> If you work for a man, in heaven's name work for him! If he pays you wages that supply you your bread and butter, work for him—speak well of him, think well of him, stand by him and stand by the institution he represents.
>
> *Elbert Hubbard*

Respect the Confidence of Subordinates

If an employee tells you something in confidence, then try to keep it in confidence. If word gets out that you violated a subordinate's trust, the future communication between you and your employees may be damaged forever.

Caution: In the modern-day workplace, some personnel laws and policies may require a supervisor who learns of a serious problem in the workplace to notify his superior, the personnel department, or a specific government agency. So if a subordinate tries to speak with you in confidence, you should warn him that you may not be able to keep certain things in strict confidence, and then give him the option of continuing to speak with you or not.

> If you once forfeit the confidence of your fellow citizens, you can never regain their respect and esteem.
>
> *Abraham Lincoln*

Chapter five is now complete. But I leave you with these last words of wisdom on the subject of confidence:

> Who has confidence in himself will gain the confidence of others.
>
> *Leib Lazarow*

CHAPTER 6

WHAT THE BEST SUPERVISORS DO

What do the best supervisors do when they are actually supervising their people? Their subordinates know the answer. After all, who sees the boss more clearly than her subordinates?

In this chapter, I'll tell you what the best supervisors do and what they are expected to do by the people they supervise and by the people who supervise them.

As you read through this chapter, keep the following question in mind: would your subordinates, peers, and bosses elect you to your present position?

> We confide in our strength, without boasting of it; we respect that of others, without fearing it.
>
> *Thomas Jefferson*

They Follow the Rules

Good supervisors do what they are told, willingly and to the best of their ability.

They pursue the goals and objectives of the organization. In all organizations, we must follow standard policies, procedures, and traditions to get the job done in an orderly and timely fashion.

We are all subordinate to someone, and good supervisors understand that.

> The high destiny of the individual is to serve rather than to rule.
>
> *Albert Einstein*

They Recognize Good Work

The best supervisors recognize good work as quickly as they recognize poor work. It is important for them to provide positive reinforcement and constructive feedback to their subordinates.

They also recognize the contribution that every member of the team makes to the success of the organization. People want approval from the boss as well as from their peers. So take the time to recognize their accomplishments and abilities.

> The deepest principle of human nature is the craving to be appreciated.
>
> *William James*

They Create Team Spirit

Good supervisors get others to join the team, to get on board, and work toward a common goal for their unit or department. People want to be a part of something larger than themselves, and with the proper motivation, they will join up because they want to.

The best supervisors then continue to lead their team to success, not for money, but for the recognition of a job well done.

The supervisor's enthusiasm for his own work will carry over to the other members of the team, who will soon have the same enthusiasm for their work.

Subordinates should ultimately look at a project and say, "Our team did this and I contributed."

> When you're part of a team, you stand up for your teammates. Your loyalty is to them. You protect them through good and bad, because they will do the same for you.
>
> *Yogi Berra*

They Encourage Cooperation

Good supervisors encourage cooperation among and between subordinates, bosses, and various other departments of the organization.

In general, all of those units are seeking the same final goal. However, that long-range, final goal is often clouded in territorialism, petty bickering, jealousies, and ego gratification.

Good supervisors encourage all of their people to get along and work together. As a result, a good supervisor can make a real difference in getting tasks and objectives accomplished with little conflict.

> Light is the task, where many share the work.
>
> *Homer*

They Expect High Quality and Quantity

Good supervisors get the high quality and quantity of work necessary for the success of their unit. And that can be difficult at times.

In general, all employees want to know what is expected of them, and good supervisors make it very clear as to what they want. They also firmly make it clear that their reasonable standards are the minimum standards expected, and that less will not be tolerated.

However, human nature being what it is, some will try to get by with doing a little less than others. Good supervisors do not tolerate substandard performance by their employees. It is not fair to the others who are working up to acceptable standards.

> Always do more than is required of you.
>
> *General George S. Patton*

They Get People Involved

Good supervisors make their people feel that it is not just a job—it is *their* job.

They ask their people for their opinions, get their perspectives, listen to their ideas, and let them be innovative. People want interesting jobs and new challenges. Help them get excited and get involved. They'll be happier and so will you.

> An automobile goes nowhere efficiently unless it has a quick, hot spark to ignite things, to set the cogs of the machine in motion. So I try to make every player on my team feel he's the spark keeping our machine in motion.
>
> *Knute Rockne*

They Don't Coddle Poor Performers

Occasionally, despite their best motivational skills, supervisors will find employees who just won't perform up to standards. They violate basic rules and will not perform as they are expected to.

Good supervisors will then try to get those employees involved, using every method they can think of, but they don't carry underperformers forever.

The best supervisors either get underperformers to follow the rules and perform up to standards, or they make other arrangements for them. Other arrangements might include transfer, reassignment, disciplinary action, or dismissal.

One poor performer, if allowed to continue in the poor performance mode, can destroy morale and undermine an entire operation.

> There is no use whatever trying to help people who do not help themselves. You cannot push anyone up a ladder unless he is willing to climb himself.
>
> *Andrew Carnegie*

They Manage Conflict

At times, reasonable people will disagree.

But conflict within a department can tear it apart. A good supervisor steps in and resolves the conflict before it has a chance to adversely affect the whole unit.

Conflict developing between departments is handled the same way—with the supervisor's equal in the other department.

Naturally the conflict must always be handled with a fair and equitable solution for all concerned. The best supervisors resolve the conflict, leaving both sides as winners when the conflict ends.

> There never was a time when, in my opinion, some way could not be found to prevent the drawing of the sword.
>
> *Ulysses S. Grant*

They Care about Their Employees

Employees are people, not machines. The best supervisors get to know and understand their people. They treat them with dignity and respect. They protect them from abuses and help them with problems. The best supervisors are understanding and accessible to their employees.

People want to work in a safe and healthy environment where they are appreciated for their skills and efforts.

The best supervisors know that their units' greatest assets are their people, and they treat them accordingly.

> The employer generally gets the employees he deserves.
>
> *Sir Walter Gilbey*

CHAPTER 7

QUICK WISDOM: SUPERVISION

In the six previous chapters on supervision, we covered a variety of topics, actions, and attitudes that supervisors need to succeed in their careers. In this last supervision chapter, I'll present two contrasting lists of traits of real-world supervisors. These lists were compiled from actual survey results of employees and supervisors.

I strongly suggest that you carefully review them and reflect on both the pros and cons of your own supervisory actions and attitudes. Consider it your opportunity to look into a supervisory mirror and evaluate what you see.

25 Traits of Excellent Supervisors

Excellent supervisors:

1. Are honest

2. Are fair

3. Give positive reinforcement

4. Are knowledgeable

5. Respect subordinates

6. Are interested in subordinates

7. Set goals

8. Set the example

9. Have common sense

10. Are decisive

11. Are teachers

12. Back subordinates' decisions

13. Are good listeners

14. Delegate work

15. Aren't Monday-morning quarterbacks

16. Are available

17. Communicate well

18. Are responsible for their own actions

19. Are consistent

20. Are willing to help

21. Take command

22. Don't hold grudges

23. Show enthusiasm for their work

24. Give constructive feedback

25. Don't overmanage

25 Traits of Poor Supervisors

Poor supervisors:

1. Close their minds

2. Are two-faced

3. Don't set a good example

4. Overmanage

5. Undermanage

6. Are insensitive to subordinates' needs

7. Don't have respect for subordinates

8. Are inconsistent

9. Don't accept responsibility for decisions

10. Are arrogant

11. Lack experience

12. Take credit for the work of others

13. Publicly criticize subordinates

14. Show favoritism

15. Fail to recognize subordinates' good work

16. Are indecisive

17. Hold grudges

18. Communicate poorly

19. Are overly critical

20. Are lazy

21. Use power to intimidate subordinates

22. Are insecure

23. Are dishonest

24. Fail to teach subordinates

25. Fail to back subordinates' decisions

> There are no secrets to success. It is the result of
> preparation, hard work, and learning
> from failure.
>
> *Colin Powell*

OK, now that you have mastered the basic art of being a successful supervisor, keep reading and find out what it takes to become a successful manager in the real world.

PART TWO

MANAGEMENT
IT'S EASY
ONCE
YOU KNOW
HOW

CHAPTER 8

YOUR INTRODUCTION TO MANAGEMENT

> Management is nothing more than motivating other people.
>
> *Lee Iacocca*

What Does a Manager Do?

A competent manager must ensure that she has the right people, in the right place, at the right time, and with all of the equipment and supplies necessary to get the job done.

Essentially that means, as a manager, you will need people skills to be sure your people are with you and will follow your direction. You will have to exercise all of the skills learned in the previous chapters on supervision to do that.

You will also need to know exactly what upper-level managers expect from your unit or department.

You will need to know where you and your people need to be, and what time to be there.

You will have to determine what equipment and supplies you need for your unit to perform the tasks required. And you will need to know where you will get those supplies and equipment.

And then?

Then you can schedule personnel and make transportation arrangements for your personnel, the supplies, and the equipment. You will also arrange to get them all together at the proper place and at the proper time, with the proper directions, orders, and motivation to get the job done. Then you must have backup plans in place in case something goes wrong along the way.

Keep in mind that, to be a good manager, you will need excellent supervisory skills. Being a great manager also means that you will be required to have good leadership skills in order to link these abilities all together and to know where you and your group are going. So supervision, management, and leadership all interact, and you will need to use many of the skills you learn from this book to be successful in your everyday actions.

You *can* do it all!

In the following pages, you will learn what skills, attitudes, and actions you will need to become a successful manager.

It may seem difficult right now, but once you know and practice the rules, it gets much easier.

CHAPTER 9

PREVENTING AND HANDLING PROBLEMS

All problems can be handled, no matter how difficult they appear to be. Your ability to foresee, prevent, and handle problems can be a true test of your skills as a manager.

The following pages will assist you in handling this sometimes difficult area of management.

> These are the times that try men's souls.
> *Thomas Paine*

Actively Supervise

You just finished several chapters on how to be a successful supervisor. I hope you learned well. But there is more that a good manager does to continue to supervise effectively.

Check on everything periodically. You can rest assured that the area you don't check will be the source of the next crisis.

Don't always take another's word for things. Get out of your office and double-check how the work is progressing. It's nice to trust, but you also have to be sure that your trust is well placed.

> Modest doubt is called the beacon of the wise.
> *William Shakespeare*

Ensure That the Goals Are Understood

Tell your employees what you want, then have them tell you what you want.

Follow up with written orders, then check to see that they understand the written orders.

Check the progress being made on the project periodically to be sure it is being done according to the intent of your directives.

Communication is an inexact art. However, making the communication as clear as possible will enhance performance and minimize errors.

> It is less dishonour to hear imperfectly, than to speak imperfectly.
>
> *Ben Johnson*

Anticipate Problem Areas

Look ahead. What areas could cause you and your unit difficulties? Possible problem areas may include the following:

- New employees
- Poor training
- Inexperience
- Poor-quality materials
- Too much, too fast—of anything

You can't see into the future, but you can project the ramifications of certain factors on the success of a project.

Correct as many deficiencies as possible before they cause problems.

> It isn't that they can't see the solution. It is that they can't see the problem.
>
> *G. K. Chesterton*

Do Something

Don't ignore a problem.

Don't try to hide it; handle it. Correct the problem and take steps to ensure it doesn't become a problem again in the future.

Many problems which could have been solved with a small amount of managerial intervention have been ignored until they ultimately escalated into a serious problem for employees, managers and the organization.

Don't let it happen to you.

> Facts do not cease to exist because they are ignored.
>
> *Aldous Huxley*

Investigate

Get all the facts about the problem that has occurred and identify the factors leading up to it.

Interview the affected or involved employees. Get their ideas on what happened, why it occurred and how it could have been prevented. Caution: Managerial interviews may be governed by management/employee agreements. Before starting interviews, know where you stand as a manager, consistent with those agreements and past practices of your organization. Some employees may have special rights under those agreements. Call your boss for advice if you are not sure where you stand in such matters.

Back up the interviews with physical evidence whenever possible. Check every source of information you can think of.

Once you gather all of the facts and you look at the whole picture, you can take sound and logical steps to correct the problem and prevent a recurrence in the future.

> To solve a problem, it is necessary to think. It is necessary to think even to decide what facts to collect.
>
> *Robert Maynard Hutchins*

Do Your Homework

After you investigate to find the cause of the problem, you can formulate possible solutions.

Take time to analyze the solutions and project what effects these possible solutions will have on your department, other departments and the organization as a whole.

Once you do your homework in this area, you will see things more logically and clearly and you'll have the answers for the boss when he starts asking his own questions.

> If a man takes no thought about what is distant, he will find sorrow near at hand.
>
> *Confucius*

Be Creative

Turn adversity into opportunity.

When a problem occurs, the most important task for a manager is to get it corrected so the operation can return to normal as soon as possible.

However, don't stop there. Stand back and look at the problem objectively. Ask yourself questions such as "How could this have been prevented?" and "What can I learn from this?"

The answers may surprise you.

Perhaps the incident will give you the support you need to get new equipment or increased training for your employees.

Creative thinking can lead to creative solutions.

> Creativeness often consists of merely turning up what is already there.
>
> *Bernie Fitz-Gibbon*

Document Your Actions

Put these facts on paper:

- How the problem came to your attention
- How you investigated the problem
- What caused the problem
- What steps you took to solve it
- What you did to prevent recurrence

Take the time to document the problem and your actions in writing. Keep the documentation on file. It will prove invaluable weeks or months later in the following:

- Employee disciplinary hearings
- Employee evaluations
- Your evaluation
- Future disciplinary hearings or lawsuits

> A memorandum is written not to inform the reader but to protect the writer.
>
> *Dean Acheson*

Don't Embarrass the Boss

Keep your supervisor informed.

Nothing could be more embarrassing than your supervisor's supervisor asking for the status of a particular problem when your supervisor has no idea that the problem even exists.

Periodically inform your supervisor of the status of your investigation into the problem area and your preliminary findings.

When you have completed your investigation, have corrected the problem, and made a list of recommendations for preventing future occurrences, contact your supervisor again.

She will appreciate your follow-up work and will know that there is no need for further action on her part.

> The past at least is secure.
> *Daniel Webster*

CHAPTER 10

BEING A GOOD ADMINISTRATOR

Along with being a manager, you are also an administrator. As an administrator you will be required to ensure that organizational policies and procedures are followed—it goes with the territory. You will be charged with keeping accurate records of supplies, equipment, maintenance, and personnel.

Keeping administrative records is just a part of being a manager, so get used to it and keep those administrative records to the best of your ability.

On the following pages, you will find a few additional tips on administrative survival to help you along your way.

> Bad administration, to be sure, can destroy good policy.
>
> *Adlai Stevenson*

Write It Down

You now have too many things on your mind to rely solely on your memory. If you don't write things down, you're going to forget to be somewhere or do something, and that will reflect adversely on you and cause problems for others.

A simple daily or weekly calendar will help keep track of appointments, events, and deadlines. Of course, you always have to remember to look at the calendar regularly.

> Quite literally, a man's memory is what he forgets with.
> *Odell Shepard*

Get Organized

When you can't find the last marketing report, the vacation schedule, shipping papers, or anything else in less than five minutes, you are in serious trouble. Continue in that pattern and soon you won't need to find anything—at least not at that job.

Take time to get organized, but not to the point of being a fanatic about it.

With a little thought, planning, and self-discipline, you can make effective use of daily scheduling guides, file folders, in- and out-baskets, computers, planning and scheduling software, and a whole host of other items.

Consider time spent getting organized—and staying organized—as job insurance.

> Let all things be done decently and in order.
> *1 Corinthians 14:40*

Manage Resources Effectively

You are responsible for the effective and efficient use of the resources at your disposal. This includes material, equipment, and the most valuable of all resources, the employees.

Ensure that you have enough resources to get the job done. Plan ahead so you have enough people, material, and equipment, all at the right time, and in the right place, to get the job done.

In addition, your job is to prevent the waste of valuable resources. This includes time as well as materials. Proper planning, coupled with proper supervision, will ensure that all resources are used effectively.

> Nothing is more terrible than activity without insight.
>
> *Thomas Carlyle*

Keep Good Records

Production records, overtime usage, attendance records, employee performance records, supply orders, equipment accountability—these are just a few of the records you may be required to keep as a manager.

Records are as necessary to the control of a business as laws are to maintaining an orderly society. Accept the fact that they must be kept and that you must keep them as accurately as possible. You will find that, with proper organization and forethought on your part, they are not all that difficult to keep.

Many administrators fail in this area because they continually put record keeping low on their list of priorities. Subsequently this activity builds up into an overwhelming, time-consuming task.

Keeping good records on a daily or weekly basis, a little at a time, will make this activity—and your job—much easier.

> Order marches with weighty and measured strides; disorder is always in a hurry.
>
> *Napoleon Bonaparte*

Delegate Tasks

You can't do everything yourself.

You have to delegate some tasks to other competent people—not just menial tasks but meaningful tasks as well.

Be sure that the person to whom you delegate the task has the ability to perform the task. Then trust him. Give him an assignment and the authority to carry it out.

But remember the cardinal rule of delegation: you can delegate authority but not responsibility. You are responsible for the end result.

> Treat people as if they were what they ought to be, and you help them become what they are capable of being.
>
> *Johann Wolfgang von Goethe*

Develop Personal Contacts

Just as people can create a myriad of problems, other people can solve a myriad of problems.

Knowing the right person to call to get an answer or to solve a problem can make your life much easier.

Take the time to get to know the union steward, the payroll clerk, the person who handles medical claims, the storeroom custodian, the personnel officer, and other people in key positions.

You'll find that the best ones want to know you and will be happy to help you when you call. They are as proud of their work and ability to get things done as you are.

Getting to know other staff members will be time well invested. They can often help you solve problems quickly—problems that otherwise might take a great deal of time and effort if you had to work through more formal channels.

> Knowing is of two kinds. We know a subject ourselves, or we know where we can find information upon it.
>
> *Samuel Johnson*

Manage Your Time

With increased responsibilities as administrators, you should get increased time to carry out those responsibilities—but you don't. Therefore you have three options:

1. You can use what time you do have to its maximum efficiency, carefully balancing among administration, management, supervision, and time for your people. It's a difficult task, but then it goes with the title you've earned.

2. You can constantly be behind—late with deadlines, always behind on paperwork, and not knowing what is going on. Of course if you choose this option, you will constantly be a nervous wreck and probably won't have your job very long.

3. You can significantly expand your workday. Work twelve to fourteen hours every day, six days a week, and take work home with you every night—and some for Sunday too. With this option, you'll keep your job, but probably lose your spouse, family, and personal identity, as well as have a heart attack at a young age.

Which option do you prefer? Even with option one, there will be times when you have to put in long days or take work home, but if you plan your time efficiently, those times will be few. The choice is up to you.

> Work expands so as to fill the time available for its completion.
>
> *Northcote Parkinson*

WINNING LOYALTY

> Too often a sense of loyalty depends on admiration, and if we can't admire, it is difficult to be loyal.
>
> *Aimee Buchanan*

Be Pleasant

Treat others as you would like to be treated. Being pleasant is easy, and it doesn't cost you anything.

Keeping the work environment comfortable for your subordinates will make them want to come to work, and they'll enjoy their stay more while they are there.

This will ultimately translate into increased productivity within your department as a direct result of your friendly demeanor.

> Be pleasant until ten o'clock in the morning and the rest of the day will take care of itself.
>
> *Elbert Hubbard*

Know Your People

Your people are your most valuable asset. However, they are individual people, not objects.

Get to know their hobbies and interests. Ask about their families, their health, their vacation. They'll know that you care about them as people, not just as employees.

Learn their strengths and their weaknesses. You will then be able to steer them in the right direction when assigning work so they can maximize their own potential.

In assigning tasks that allow them to use their talents and abilities without exceeding their capabilities, you will develop a satisfied and loyal employee.

> There is no meaning to life except the meaning man gives his life by the unfolding of his powers.
>
> *Erich Fromm*

Help Your People to Do Their Jobs

Make their work easier for them by providing them with training, experience, or new technology.

Be sure that they have all of the proper tools to do their jobs to the best of their abilities.

Eliminate any stumbling blocks to the successful completion of their tasks. These obstacles may be unreasonable restrictions or deadlines, or a lack of proper resources, or may come from other departments.

And, of course, give employees the encouragement they need to successfully complete difficult or lengthy tasks.

> So much of what we call management consists of making it difficult for people to work.
>
> *Peter Drucker*

Train Your People

They can't do a good job for you unless they know how. Show them the proper way of doing the job they are assigned to do.

Tell people what you expect in regard to productivity. Take time with them until they have learned the job thoroughly. After that, teach them new or easier ways of doing their jobs.

Encourage employees to learn new skills, either on or off the job. In fact, arrange for it by making them aware of schools, seminars, training sessions, and new technology.

Learning new skills will keep employees from becoming stagnant. It will lead to your being able to rely on them for new projects or to take on increased responsibility.

Training is beneficial to them, to you, and to the organization.

> To teach is to learn.
>
> *Japanese Proverb*

Develop Your People

Take time to talk to them about their futures.

Give your people the benefit of your experience and advise them on how to succeed in their own careers.

If they show talent in a particular area, assist them in gaining additional knowledge and experience in that area.

Give them added responsibility gradually. Build up their confidence and ability.

The time you spend will pay dividends in their increased performance—now and in the future.

After all, didn't someone during your career take the time to talk to you, train you, and tell you how to be successful?

> Few things help an individual more than to place responsibility upon him, and to let him know that you trust him.
>
> *Booker T. Washington*

Watch Out for Your People

Protect them from unreasonable rules or poor decisions that adversely affect them.

Assist employees in obtaining their medical and dental benefits, tuition assistance, special training, and so on.

Help employees get time off when they need it for personal affairs.

If they make an error, help to minimize the effect of that error. That will also minimize the consequences they may face, such as disciplinary action or a poor performance rating.

If you watch out for your employees, they will watch out for you.

> You must be able to underwrite the honest mistakes of your subordinates if you wish to develop their initiative and experience.
>
> *General Bruce C. Clarke*

Maintain Safety Standards

Protect your people. Keep safety equipment available and in good working condition. Ensure that your people know how to use the equipment properly. Enforce the safety rules rigidly.

The supervisor who forges ahead to meet production quotas at the expense of safety, clearly shows employees that she doesn't care about them as people.

If you don't care about them, do you think they will care about you?

> If you are out of trouble, watch for danger.
>
> *Sophocles*

Be Understanding

Try to understand your subordinates' problems. Listen to them.

You are not just a boss: you are the symbol of something stronger and, they feel, wiser than they are. Therefore, they will value your opinion in all matters.

Assist your people whenever you can by listening and/or counseling. As a result of your attention, they will often solve their own problems, answer their own questions, and make their own decisions, sometimes without you having to say a word.

> To say the right thing at the right time, keep still most of the time.
>
> *John W. Roper*

The Value of Loyalty

The dedication of your employees can be critical to your future success within your organization.

Never forget that as you go higher in the organization, many of your best employees will also go higher in the organization.

The old adage "Surround thyself with competence" may take on new meaning if you need competent and dedicated employees to support you when you go on to a new position.

In many circumstances, the loyalties built up in the past can be invaluable in the future.

> Be nice to people on your way up because you may meet them on your way down.
>
> *Anonymous*

CHAPTER 12

WHAT THE BEST MANAGERS DO

The best managers recognize that only a limited number of goals can be pursued at any one time. Therefore they must accurately determine what is important and what is less important.

The most important priorities receive the first attention. Then everything else follows in descending order of importance.

Meeting a deadline on a trivial matter is good, but not when a major project is put hopelessly behind as a result.

Good managers must use their judgment, after gathering all the facts and analyzing them, to be sure that all of their priorities are in the right place.

> It is best to do things systematically, since we are only humans, and disorder is our worst enemy.
>
> *Hesiod*

They Think Multifacetedly

The best managers are able to handle a variety of projects at one time.

Their thoughts are organized into a series of channels. They are able to select the correct channel, tune their mind to it, immediately evaluate the status of it, and then receive or give information about it.

If the next phone call or other input is about another project, they switch to the appropriate channel and effectively handle the situation.

The manager who can only think about one thing or one project will have great difficulty in being promoted to a higher position in the future.

> I do not feel obliged to believe that the same God who has endowed us with sense, reason, and intellect has intended us to forego their use.
>
> *Galileo Galilei*

They Use Good Judgment

Basic judgment skills should be honed by education, training, and years of diversified experience.

All of these factors will combine to allow good managers to gather the facts, analyze them, project solutions, evaluate them, and arrive at a decision that is fair and sound for all concerned.

> Reason and judgment are the qualities of a leader.
>
> *Tacitus*

They Diagnose Well

The best managers can analyze the facts quickly to prevent or solve a problem.

Their research, knowledge, and experience allow them to know the system so well that dealing with it is often second nature.

Like well-trained mechanics, they can identify a problem and correct it before it gets worse.

> Life is short, art long, opportunity fleeting, experience treacherous, judgment difficult.
>
> *Hippocrates*

They Ask for Input

The best managers ask for input from:

- Subordinates
- Peers
- Superiors
- Outside sources

The best managers recognize that no single person can have all of the answers all of the time. They also know that they can always learn from others.

> There are no problems we cannot solve together, and very few that we can solve by ourselves.
>
> *Lyndon Baines Johnson*

They Make Decisions

To be considered a good manager without having the fortitude to make sound decisions in a timely fashion is unthinkable.

There is no place for the faint of heart when it comes to decision making. Decision avoidance is unacceptable.

Some decisions are better than others, but the best managers make very few wrong decisions. They call upon their years of education, training, and experience to make the best decisions possible.

Managers may also have to implement unpopular decisions made at, or above, their level. The best managers do it in such a way that their subordinates understand that the decision has been made and that it must be carried out.

> The whole world steps aside for the man who knows where he is going.
>
> *Anonymous*

They Handle Frustration Well

On a daily basis, managers deal with numerous people, many of whom will make conflicting demands on them, their people, and their resources.

Incompetent managers become frustrated and seriously stressed. However, competent leaders will sort things out, set priorities, and get done what they can.

The best managers develop the ability to accept those things that they do not have the power or the ability to change. Then they move on.

> I sit here all day trying to persuade people to do the thing they ought to have sense enough to do without my persuading them.
>
> *Harry S. Truman*

They Handle Stress Well

Directly related to frustration is the stress that results from it. Along with other daily problems, managers can face a great deal of stress.

But the best managers become cooler when the heat is turned up. For them, stress merely arouses their competitive spirit, allowing them to think more clearly and quickly, and to act decisively.

> The ultimate measure of a man is not where he stands in moments of comfort and convenience, but where he stands at times of challenge and controversy.
>
> *Martin Luther King Jr.*

They Expedite

The best managers keep the work from getting bogged down.

When a lack of supplies threatens to slow production, they expedite the arrival of the needed supplies.

When bureaucratic red tape threatens to adversely affect their people or their unit, they cut through the red tape to keep things moving.

The best managers ensure that everybody has what they need to get the job done when they need it, whether that be supplies, people, cooperation, or guidance.

> We can lick gravity, but sometimes the paperwork is overwhelming.
>
> *Werner von Braun*

They Run Effective Meetings

Too many managerial hours are spent in long, boring, marginally productive meetings.

However, if you must have meetings, they should always:

- Start on time
- Have a definite agenda
- End as quickly as possible

Then get everyone back to what they do best: working!

From your boss's perspective, if you can't run an effective meeting, what can you run?

> The length of a meeting rises with the square of the number of people present.
>
> *Eileen Shanahan*

They Communicate Very Well

The best managers have very good communication skills.

Their communications, both written and verbal, are clear and concise.

The best managers follow up verbal communications with written communications so that there are no misunderstandings.

They speak and write in terms of the education, maturity level, and experience of the recipient so they can be easily understood.

> Communication is something so simple and difficult that we can never put it in simple words.
>
> *T. S. Matthews*

They Keep Their Lives in Balance

In order to be considered a successful person, you must be successful in a variety of areas. Some of the more important, and often conflicting, areas are job, family, public service, church, social life, and recreation.

The best managers balance their lives, using their energies and skills in a variety of places, not just the work environment.

Balance all facets of your life to enjoy it to the fullest.

> No pleasure endures, unseasoned by variety.
> *Publilius Syrus*

CHAPTER 13

QUICK WISDOM: MANAGEMENT

If you have been reading straight through this book, you have gained valuable insight into what it takes to be a successful supervisor as well as a successful manager.

And it is almost time for you to start learning how to go to the next level to become a successful *leader* in your chosen profession.

But before you do that, please take a few minutes to review the list below of twenty-five common mistakes that have been made by new managers. The list comes from an actual survey of working people who are active employees, supervisors, or managers.

The new managers who made these mistakes may not have had the opportunity for the training and insight you are receiving.

Review them carefully, just to be sure that you don't make these mistakes when you are promoted to the position of manager in your organization.

25 Common Mistakes Made by New Managers

These new managers:

1. Made changes for the sake of change
2. Immediately made drastic changes in discipline or procedures
3. Were unable to effectively deal with people
4. Failed to take charge of the department
5. Made serious administrative errors

6. Tried to be "one of the guys"

7. Did subordinates' work for them

8. Failed to delegate

9. Gave no positive reinforcement to subordinates

10. Had an inconsistent approach to problems

11. Failed to listen to subordinates

12. Failed to solicit input from subordinates

13. Showed favoritism among subordinates

14. Failed to motivate subordinates

15. Didn't address problems of subordinates

16. Failed to make timely decisions

17. Failed to effectively utilize time

18. Lacked communication skills

19. Didn't know contents of required paperwork

20. Failed to foster positive interdepartmental relations

21. Failed to document positive and negative activities of subordinates

22. Gave only negative criticism

23. Failed to deal with problems immediately

24. Didn't know when to seek advice from or to advise superiors of problems

25. Lacked knowledge of labor laws, contracts, or procedures

> Success is not final, failure is not fatal: it is the courage to continue that counts.
> *Winston Churchill*

Just as good managers do many of the same things that good supervisors do, you will soon find that good leaders do many of the same things good managers and supervisors do. But leaders set themselves apart from the ordinary supervisor or manager. Read on to find out how.

> Management is doing things right; leadership is doing the right things.
>
> *Peter Drucker*

PART THREE

LEADERSHIP
THERE IS
A WAY TO
SUCCESS

CHAPTER 14

YOUR INTRODUCTION TO LEADERSHIP

You have now reached the stage where you have learned to effectively supervise the work of others. You have also learned to manage people, things, and time. Now it is time for you to free yourself to become a successful leader.

In this section, you will learn skills that set leaders apart from supervisors and managers. There is a big difference between people who want to get a promotion and pay raise and those who want to lead a group to do new, innovative, and exciting things.

Leaders have vision. They look out on the horizon and see where they and their unit and organization need to go. Then they share that vision with their people. Next they get their people excited about reaching that vision. They also have the skills to get a commitment from their people to develop that vision with enthusiasm and a team spirit.

Are you up to the challenge of earning that elusive title of leader?

If you think you are, read on.

> Leadership is action, not position.
> *Donald H. McGannon*

Can Anyone Lead?

Not just anyone.

However, those who have the desire to lead, who are willing to make the commitment to being a leader, and who prepare themselves properly can become a leader, with very few exceptions.

Leadership requires the knowledge necessary to understand the leadership role, the training to perform the day-to-day activities required of a leader, and a sound foundation of experience upon which to base future decisions.

This preparation is absolutely necessary, but the most important quality necessary to be a leader is desire:

- The desire to lead the way
- The desire to take on difficult problems
- The desire to go a step beyond
- And, of course, the desire to be a leader of others

> Leaders learn by leading, and they learn best by leading in the face of obstacles. As weather shapes mountains, problems shape leaders.
>
> *Walter Bennis*

What Is Leadership?

Leadership is the art of influencing and directing people in such a way as to obtain their confidence, respect, and cooperation. Anyone can be boss, but the person who has personnel working with, rather than for or under, him is the true leader of people.

Your leadership responsibilities will include the accomplishment of organization objectives and the welfare of your organization's personnel.

You must satisfy subordinates, peers, and superiors. Keep in mind that you can't lead by yourself: you need someone to follow you.

You don't have to be a genius to be a leader. Most leaders are people of slightly above-average intelligence.

Leadership is not a mysterious phenomenon. It is a combination of skills and observable behaviors that can be learned. This section of the book can help you to learn those skills and behaviors.

What Do Leaders Do?

There is an enormous difference between those who want to squirt oil on the machinery and those who want to build new machinery. Strong leadership can help design and build that new machinery with innovative features and outstanding workmanship.

Leaders get people excited! They build on strengths rather than dwelling on weaknesses. People will then willingly sign up to serve under outstanding leaders.

Truly effective leaders combine supervisory, managerial, and leadership skills to get the best from their people and themselves. Supervisors, managers, and leaders share some of the same tasks, but it is the way they perform them and the way they treat the people involved that distinguishes leaders from the rest of the pack.

As an example, supervisors supervise and managers control, but leaders create commitment and are absolutely essential in times of chaos, crisis, or change. When things are running routinely, a manager can maintain the status quo. But when there is a crisis, somebody has to take charge. That's the leader!

While supervisors and managers cover the more technical aspects of business, such as getting the basic tasks done, leaders are people with inspiration and vision. Leaders are inspired by their desire to succeed at the tasks ahead of them. Their vision allows them to see what needs to be done for their unit to succeed. When they share both their vision and inspirations with their people, everyone, including the organization, moves ahead.

Leaders take exceptional pride in their own accomplishments, as well as the accomplishments of their people and the unit they lead.

> Effective leadership is not about making speeches or being liked; leadership is defined by results . . .
>
> *Peter Drucker*

Can You Be a Leader?

Leadership can be learned. Reading the following pages can get you started down one of the most exciting roads you will ever travel. Good luck.

> The difference between a boss and a leader: a boss says, "Go"—a leader says, "Let's go!"
>
> *E. M. Kelly*

CHAPTER 15

LEADERS PREPARE BY . . .

Preparing yourself to be a leader can be as critical to your future success as any subsequent actions you may take. Several tips in this chapter tell you how to prepare yourself for the leadership role. Read them carefully.

If you don't believe that adequate preparation is necessary, just read what our panel of experts has to say:

> The man who is prepared has his battle half-fought.
>
> *Cervantes*

> I will prepare and someday my chance will come.
>
> *Abraham Lincoln*

> Before everything else, getting ready is the secret of success.
>
> *Henry Ford*

Mastering the Basics

A leader must possess many qualities and master many skills. Which leadership qualities and skills do you already possess? Which do you lack? Which can you learn?

In the first two sections of this book I have given you insight into the basics of supervision and management, and now I will give you a sound foundation for successful leadership.

> Leadership is a combination of strategy and character. If you must be without one, be without the strategy.
>
> *General H. Norman Schwarzkopf*

Learning from the Past

Leadership is not new.

Leadership successes and failures have been going on since humans discovered fire (and occasionally got burned).

In this section, we continue to take advantage of the wisdom of the ages whenever possible. The words of wisdom from dozens of successful leaders throughout the centuries will help us to comprehend and remember the skills necessary for our own leadership successes.

> The farther back you can look, the farther forward you are likely to see.
>
> *Winston Churchill*

Gaining Knowledge

Knowledge of your industry and the various components which make up that industry is absolutely necessary for success.

You must have a high degree of technical competence to be successful.

You must study your industry from an intellectual as well as a practical perspective to get the big picture of your industry and its relationship to the rest of the world.

Leaders read trade magazines, newsletters, and related publications. They belong to professional organizations and attend professional trade shows, educational seminars, and appropriate social functions.

Leaders strive to be the most knowledgeable and professional people in their field.

> Leadership and learning are indispensable to each other.
>
> *John F. Kennedy*

Developing a Varied Background

Leaders develop a broad-based background of knowledge and experience they can draw from when necessary.

They develop this background by actively participating in sports, social organizations, church activities, and charity work. All of these activities can help build organizational skills, people skills, and confidence for the leader.

Leaders interact with other people. They participate in business discussions and activities, and they gain knowledge and experience in design, production, marketing, sales, and delivery systems.

> Since we cannot be universal and know all that is to be known of everything, we ought to know a little about everything.
>
> *Blaise Pascal*

Gaining Experience

Prospective leaders gain practical experience in their own or related fields.

They make an extra effort to gain more experience than their peers by getting involved.

They can then draw on diverse experiences from a variety of sources as they prepare for the future. They are always willing to take on new projects, use new techniques and technology, as well as working with other people and groups in various activities.

> However much thou art read in theory, if thou hast no practice thou art ignorant.
>
> *Sa'di*

Staying up to Date

Leaders know about and utilize the latest in new technology and procedures.

Leaders are aware of trends within their own industry, the nation, and the world.

By belonging to professional associations and reading journals, newsletters, and other publications, leaders can prepare to be on the leading edge of new technology.

The closer you are to the future, the easier it is to predict the future.

> Destiny is not a matter of chance; it is a matter of choice. It is not something to be waited for, but rather something to be achieved.
>
> *William Jennings Bryan*

Sharing Internal Information

Within your own organization, you can draw on the knowledge and resources of other people and departments to enhance your own unit's performance. Prepare for the future by initiating and cultivating personal relationships with your counterparts in other areas so you can share resources and information with them.

Some of the other departments with which you may want to share information include marketing, sales, manufacturing, customer service, personnel, and finance.

> Coming together is a beginning; keeping together is progress; working together is success.
>
> *Henry Ford*

Obtaining Outside Information

Relying solely on internal information is not enough for a leader to develop the vision needed to lead the way to future success for his unit or organization.

Leaders are the key to bringing outside information into an organization. They meet with other executives, participate in trade shows and meetings, meet and talk with customers, suppliers, and people in related industries to find out what is—or should be—new in their industry and what they can learn from other industries.

They recognize that they must improve faster and better than their competitors to remain the best.

> Knowledge and human power are synonymous.
>
> *Francis Bacon*

Becoming Good Public Speakers

Some people come by this skill naturally, but not many. Most have to learn it.

It is not hard. Most adult education programs and colleges have a course for beginners.

When you must speak in public, always:

- Be prepared
- Know your audience
- Speak from prepared notes (in case you lose your focus during your speech)
- Be positive and confident in your presentation

> Speech is power: speech is to persuade, to convert, to compel.
>
> *Ralph Waldo Emerson*

Winning Loyalty

Leaders must be able to garner the support of their subordinates and bosses in order to be successful.

Loyalty must be earned. It is earned by caring about and protecting both subordinates and bosses. It is earned by working with people and helping them to be successful.

The loyalty and dedication of subordinates can help leaders to meet difficult deadlines or solve difficult problems. The loyalty of a boss can get leaders out of potential trouble or help minimize errors.

Over time, leaders who have proven that they are worthy of subordinates' and bosses' support will have great loyalty from all.

> Loyalty is the one thing a leader cannot do without.
>
> *A. P. Goethey*

Developing a Sense of Humor

Humor is important to help keep things in perspective, for both leaders and their subordinates.

A sense of humor can ease tensions during difficult times and a little humor can help brighten anyone's day.

> A sense of humor is part of the art of leadership, of getting along with people, of getting things done.
>
> *Dwight D. Eisenhower*

CHAPTER 16

LEADERS ARE . . .

Successful leaders possess many attributes. Virtually all of them can be learned.

The following pages list attributes you should work on if being a leader is your goal.

> In the great mass of our people there are plenty of individuals of intelligence from among whom leadership can be recruited.
>
> *Herbert Hoover*

Dependable

Leaders are dependable.

Leaders keep promises, are always on time, and can be relied upon to fulfill any duty or obligation.

> A little neglect may breed great mischief . . .
> for the want of a shoe the horse was lost;
> and for the want of a horse the rider was lost.
>
> *Benjamin Franklin*

Courageous

Both physically and morally, leaders must have the personal courage to try something new:

- To go where others fear to tread
- To face adversity and to support their people
- To protect their subordinates from unfairness
- To stand up to their superiors whenever necessary

> It is courage, courage, courage that raises the blood of life to crimson splendor.
>
> *George Bernard Shaw*

Tactful

Leaders think before they speak.

Tact should be used with subordinates, bosses, customers, and suppliers.

Being tactful costs nothing but may be rewarded many times over in goodwill and solid relationships.

> Tact: the ability to describe others as they see themselves.
>
> *Abraham Lincoln*

Unselfish

Leaders always share, or give away, credit for successes.

Leaders give of their time to others to make their jobs and lives easier.

In everything they do, they exhibit the attitude of sharing, except when things go wrong. Then the true leader accepts the blame and shares it with no one.

> He who wishes to secure the good of others, has already secured his own.
>
> *Confucius*

Humble

Leaders live for success, yet they should be humble when the accolades start to flow. Being humble means being able to control one's feelings of elation and acting in a modest manner about the unit's success.

True leaders say, "Thank you" for compliments and point to their subordinates and say, "They did it."

Leaders have egos, but they keep them under control. Repeated successes can inflate leaders' egos to the point where they may think that they are invincible. The wise leader avoids this trap, for one never knows what the future may bring in terms of success or failure.

> A hundred times a day I remind myself that my life depends on the labors of other men, living and dead, and that I must exert myself in order to give, in the measure as I have received, and am still receiving.
>
> *Albert Einstein*

Optimistic

Leaders view each day as full of challenges that are a pleasure to meet and conquer.

Leaders always view a cup as being half full, not half empty. They know that planning and organization, coupled with good personnel, properly directed by a true leader, will always lead to success.

Repeatedly making all the right moves makes optimism come naturally.

> A leader is a dealer in hope.
>
> *Napoleon Bonaparte*

Creative

Leaders develop new and innovative solutions to problems.

No problem is too great.

No solution is impossible to find.

Thinking creatively is the leader's stock in trade.

In thinking creatively, a true leader dares to be bold.

> There is one thing stronger than all the armies in the world, and that is an idea whose time has come.
>
> *Victor Hugo*

Energetic

Leaders target the task at hand, then focus all their energies toward the successful attainment of that goal.

When the task is complete, leaders rest their energy momentarily, until the next task appears.

Leaders must have strong personal energy to get a project up and running. They must also maintain that energy to see projects through to completion.

> Energy and persistence conquer all things.
>
> *Benjamin Franklin*

Intelligent

Leaders have above-average intelligence but not necessarily much above average.

Leaders must have the ability to analyze, evaluate, and comprehend. To do so requires basic intelligence coupled with hard work, dedication, and commitment to the task at hand.

Once committed, leaders can overshadow people with greater intelligence because they use their resources to the fullest.

> The man who acquires the ability to take full possession of his own mind may take possession of anything else to which he is justly entitled.
>
> *Andrew Carnegie*

Honest

Scrupulously honest!

They never consider cheating or fraud. Their integrity is unquestioned.

Their peers, subordinates, bosses, and competitors know it, and respect and trust them as a result.

> No public man can be just a little crooked.
>
> *Herbert Hoover*

Consistent

No hot and cold here!

Their subordinates always know what to expect. Their peers always know what to expect. Their bosses always know what to expect.

In leadership, the best surprise is no surprise, for subordinates, peers, and bosses alike.

> We are what we repeatedly do.
>
> *Aristotle*

Loyal

Leaders are loyal to:

- Their subordinates
- Their organization
- Their bosses

We're not talking about *blind* loyalty. In order to be loyal to any person, group, or organization, a leader must evaluate the circumstances of any situation. Perhaps the best test is to ask the question, do they deserve my loyalty in this situation?

Occasionally loyalty even means constructive disagreement with a boss or a subordinate, for the good of all. A good leader knows that loyalty is a two-way street.

> An ounce of loyalty is worth a pound of cleverness.
>
> *Elbert Hubbard*

Mature

When the lives and livelihoods of others are at stake, there is no room for rash action or petty bickering.

Leaders, whatever their age, must be mature enough to face challenges and handle consequences in a cool and professional manner.

Emotional maturity is exhibited by leaders who are neither crushed by defeat nor overly elated by victory.

> Think like a man of action, act like a man of thought.
>
> *Henri-Louis Bergson*

Sincere

There can be no false pretenses here.

If a leader tells a subordinate that she did a good job, then it must have been good.

Insincerity destroys the credibility of leaders and renders them ineffective.

Always be sincere and warm.

> Sincerity is the highest compliment you can pay.
> *Ralph Waldo Emerson*

Adaptive

Change is welcomed by a true leader, even in midstream.

Human beings can adapt to almost anything, if they want to. Leaders ensure that others see the need to adapt or change, and they help them through the transition.

Leaders build a degree of flexibility into their plans to allow for unexpected changes. Leaders are willing to make changes when they are warranted.

> The unexpected always happens.
> *Lawrence J. Peters*

Tenacious

Leaders don't let go.

They keep striving toward success until it is obtained.

If their idea didn't fly this year, it will be presented again next year, and it will be even better.

Ultimately their tenacity will endure and their vision will be realized.

> There is no failure except in no longer trying.
> *Kin Hubbard*

Personable

Leaders are friendly, not arrogant or egotistical.

They are as friendly with the janitors as they are with the chairman of the board.

Leaders are open enough so that everyone around them can get to know and trust them.

Leaders are also approachable. Anyone can talk to true leaders and present a problem or idea to them without ridicule or repercussions.

True leaders are recognized as warm and likeable people.

> You can make more friends in two months by becoming interested in other people than you can in two years by trying to get other people interested in you.
> *Dale Carnegie*

Fair

Leaders are fair to everyone:

- Subordinates
- Customers
- Coworkers
- The organization
- Themselves

> To thine own self be true; and it must follow,
> as the night the day, thou canst not then be false
> to any man.
>
> *William Shakespeare*

Patient

Patience has long been lauded as a great virtue. It remains so in today's hectic world.

Leaders who exhibit patience with all whom they encounter will gain lasting respect.

> He that can have patience, can have what
> he will.
>
> *Benjamin Franklin*

LEADERS UNDERSTAND . . .

Supervisors and managers follow policies, guidelines, and rules. They know what should be done, and they do it, but often without fully understanding why they are following the rules or doing the work they are assigned.

Leaders, on the other hand, understand all of the components of the system, how they interact, and how success by each component results in the overall success of a project. They understand why the rules are the rules, and why the policies and procedures are necessary.

That kind of total understanding should be your goal if you wish to be a true leader.

> There is a great difference between knowing and understanding: you can know a lot about something and not really understand it.
>
> *Charles F. Ketterin*

The Leadership Role

Leaders understand their role as leaders. They understand that they are needed. Without good leaders, little of consequence could be accomplished.

Successful leaders enjoy their leadership role.

They find it satisfying to watch people learn, grow, and succeed under their leadership.

True leaders understand that leadership is an attitude and that the more their employees succeed, the more enjoyable it is to be a leader.

> It's not work if you love what you are doing.
> *Malcolm Forbes*

The Organization

Leaders understand:

- The structure of it
- The purpose of it
- Its role and position in the industry
- Who does what, and why they do it

Most of all, leaders understand where they fit into the organizational structure.

> No man ever looks at the world with pristine eyes. He sees it edited by a definite set of customs and institutions and ways of thinking.
> *Ruth Benedict*

The Boss

Everyone has a boss, even a leader.

Understanding that the boss wants to get the job done, with as few problems as possible, can help guide a leader to take the necessary actions to get the job done right.

Of course, a leader also understands that the boss needs to be kept informed and never wants to be embarrassed.

> Before you have an argument with your boss, you'd better take a good look at both sides—his side and the outside.
>
> *Unknown*

The Employees

Leaders study their employees' needs and desires.

Here is the short course in understanding what employees really work for:

- Appreciation of the work they do
- Being a part of something
- Being respected and understood
- Job security
- Good wages
- Interesting work
- Personal growth and/or promotions
- Good working conditions
- Emotional security and stability
- A sense of personal power

Stop and think about these ten items. Aren't they the same things that you want?

> Leadership is the art of getting somebody else to do something you want done because he wants to do it.
>
> *Dwight D. Eisenhower*

The Goals

Organizational goals come in at least three types:

1. Short-term
2. Intermediate
3. Long-term

Understanding the goals of the organization, of your unit, and of the people surrounding you will help you reach those goals.

Leaders also understand their own goals and how to reach them. All of your decisions must be made with those goals in mind.

You must never lose sight of your personal and organizational goals. You must relentlessly pursue them at all times.

> The person who makes a success of living is the one who seeks his goal steadily and aims for it unswervingly.
> *Cecil B. DeMille*

The Rules

Knowing the rules is not enough. Anyone who can memorize the Pledge of Allegiance can learn a set of rules.

The important thing is to know why the rules exist and how they came to be.

Every organization has a different set of rules. That alone should tell you something. Look at the rules of your organization in light of its history and culture.

What is the goal of a particular rule? What are the consequences to the unit if it is broken?

Asking these questions and examining the answers will help you develop an understanding of why the rules are the rules, and the importance of following them for both you and your employees.

> The man who commands efficiently must have obeyed others in the past, and the man who obeys dutifully is worthy of being some day a commander.
>
> *Cicero*

Power

The concept of power is interesting. Power can be used and abused. Power is the influence one person has over another individual or group. That power may stem from a position of authority (being one's supervisor) or from superior knowledge or personal bearing.

A leader understands its sources—how to get power and how to keep that power.

Don't confuse force with power: a million troops in a war is force; however, a disapproving look from your boss is power.

A capable leader understands this use of power.

He understands what makes the powerful, powerful. A leader also understands that the perception of power is often as great as, or greater than, having the actual power itself.

A true leader is also very careful to use his own power sparingly, if at all. Be sensitive to where power exists in your organization if you wish to be a successful leader.

> Nearly all men can stand adversity, but if you want to test a man's character, give him power.
>
> *Abraham Lincoln*

Politics

Politics: who is saying what, to whom, and why? You don't have to play politics, as long as you acknowledge the existence of the political structure and understand that politics has a substantial and sometimes subtle influence on nearly every phase of human interaction.

A leader must be cognizant of the internal and external politics involved in running any type of organization. Failure to understand these politics has been the downfall of many otherwise very capable individuals.

Fact: the higher one goes in an organization, the more politically astute one must become in order to survive.

> Knowledge of human nature is the beginning,
> and the end, of political education.
>
> *Henry Adams*

Discipline

Leaders understand the concepts of both positive and negative discipline. Positive discipline is the act of ensuring that employees know and conform to standard policies and procedures of the organization or unit. When an employee refuses to follow such policies and procedures, they may face a negative disciplinary action or sanction.

Leaders understand the necessity of discipline, and the reasons for maintaining it.

One can always tell an individual who understands discipline because that person is also a very disciplined individual. Employees want fair and reasonable discipline in the workplace and a leader who can use negative discipline sparingly.

> Speak softly, and carry a big stick—you will go far.
>
> *Theodore Roosevelt*

Timing

If showing up is 90 percent of life, then showing up at the right time is the other 10 percent.

Leaders with a good sense of timing know:

- When to speak
- When to shut up
- When to push a point
- When to back off

True leaders know when to express an opinion and when to wait until they are asked.

> To every thing there is a season, and a time to every purpose under the heaven.
>
> *Ecclesiastes 3:1*

Morale

Good morale is critical to the well-being of any work unit.

Morale is primarily a local issue. Yes, policies of the administration and other outside influences can have some effect on it, but the leader of the individual unit, by far, has the greatest influence on the morale of subordinates.

A leader's day-to-day actions and attitudes are critical. When a leader is fair, professional, and optimistic, morale in the unit will be good. Good morale leads to success, and success leads to better morale.

> When dealing with people, remember you are not dealing with creatures of logic, but with creatures of emotions, creatures bristled with prejudice and motivated by pride and vanity.
>
> *Dale Carnegie*

Limitations

Leaders understand their own limitations, but they are not necessarily limited by them.

As an example, budgets can limit available resources, but a true leader will find a way to get the job done with the resources available. Staffing three shifts can't be done with only two people, but a true leader will make the most efficient use of those two people to cover the shifts.

Time is always a limitation. Yet a true leader will make the most efficient use of the time available. Luckily there are some things that know no limits, such as:

- Dreams
- Human ingenuity
- Love

Even though you may not be able to conquer the whole world, you can comfortably conquer a small part of it, even taking into account many of your limitations.

> Problems are only opportunities in work clothes.
>
> *Henry J. Kaiser*

Mistakes

In an imperfect world, mistakes and their ensuing problems are inevitable.

Often it's a matter of when, not if, mistakes will occur.

When mistakes occur, leaders become experts in damage control, getting things back on track as soon as possible and minimizing the effect of the error. Leaders must always be willing to correct and minimize the damage caused by the honest errors of their subordinates.

True leaders tolerate, and sometimes even encourage, honest mistakes. Why? Because innovation and imagination should have no set boundaries. Some of the greatest discoveries of all time were "mistakes."

> Results! Why, man, I have gotten a lot of results. I know several thousand things that won't work.
>
> *Thomas A. Edison*

Empathy

Empathy is the ability to understand another person's situation.

Stop and think about someone else's goals, motivations, feelings, and concerns.

Once you understand your subordinates' position and why they are in it, you will be in a much better position to lead them in the proper direction.

> A man always has two reasons for doing anything—a good reason and the real reason.
>
> *J. P. Morgan*

Humor

In times of crisis, leaders must reduce a problem to real-world standards. Although there may be a serious problem in the workplace that needs immediate attention, a leader must put the crisis in context with the world outside of the workplace. They see the comedy of the situation and clear the stress and tension from the air through their own sense of humor.

Subordinates need this type of release in order to relax, reevaluate, and reprioritize their goals. Then they can refocus on what really needs to be done to correct the problem and get the job done.

The simple humor relief created by a leader can be the difference between success and failure. A true leader understands that.

> Humor is an affirmative of dignity, a declaration of man's superiority to all that befalls him.
>
> *Romain Gary*

The Future

The future represents what is new. It represents change and innovation. It represents hope and the results of past efforts and attitudes.

The present is important, and we must learn from the past. But the future provides a vision not yet attained—a target to aim for. A leader understands the importance of that vision for success.

> I like the dreams of the future better than the history of the past.
>
> *Thomas Jefferson*

CHAPTER 18

LEADERS AVOID . . .

There are certain things in the real world that can cancel out all of your preparations and good intentions for becoming a success at any level.

In this chapter I present a host of them. Avoid them if you want to be successful.

> This is a hard and precarious world, where every mistake and infirmity must be paid for in full.
>
> *Clarence Day*

Being Late

For anything.

If you show up late for a meeting, you waste not only your time but that of others as well. In any industry, time is money.

If you are late in the morning, take extended breaks or two-hour lunches, your employees will follow your example.

> Dost thou love life? Then do not squander time, for that is the stuff life is made of.
>
> *Benjamin Franklin*

Overspecialization

In general, managers and leaders have a wide variety of knowledge on many subjects. Even though they may also have a specialty area, they avoid overspecialization.

Overspecialization in one area tends to make a person a technician rather than a leader of technicians.

> The world's great men have not commonly been great scholars, nor its great scholars great men.
>
> *Oliver Wendell Holmes*

Blaming Others

When in a position of power, everything that occurs is your responsibility, even the errors.

Rather than spending effort in placing the blame on others, your job is to minimize the damage and to take the steps necessary so that the problem does not reoccur in the future.

> The buck stops here!
> *Harry S. Truman*

Criticism of Others

Successful people find the strong points of individuals and focus on those.

Openly criticizing subordinates is a counterproductive activity since they will not want to perform for a critic.

Openly criticizing superiors is a sure way to shorten your career in that organization.

> He that is without sin among you, let him first cast a stone.
> *John 8:7*

Jealousy

Successful people focus on their own career and accomplishments.

Others, including those in competition with you, will also garner accomplishments and awards. Rather than wasting energy on jealousy, share their joy of accomplishment. Seek them out as friends and colleagues. Learn from them.

Winners associate with winners.

> Of all the passions, jealousy is that which exerts the hardest service and pays the bitterest wages.
>
> *Charles Caleb Colton*

Excessive Pressure

Successful people avoid receiving or giving excessive pressure.

Set realistic goals for yourself and your subordinates. Too often standards are set too high or timetables are unrealistically short to accomplish the task at hand.

If an unrealistic task is given to you, realize it and present the facts to your boss to show that his expectations should be modified.

Excessive pressure on employees serves no purpose and often kills initiative and creativity at all levels.

> We are more often frightened than hurt; our troubles spring more often from fancy than reality.
>
> *Seneca*

Union Conflicts

If you have a union or unions in your workplace, preparation and fundamental fairness are your best allies to avoid problems in this area.

Read and understand the union contracts of everyone in your work unit. Then follow them to the letter.

Unions developed in response to management abuses. If you treat everyone as you would like to be treated, follow the contracts to the letter, and know the past practices of your organization, you will avoid conflicts with union representatives.

> It is one of the characteristics of a free and democratic modern nation that it have free and independent labor unions.
>
> *Franklin D. Roosevelt*

Second-Guessing

Subordinates should be encouraged to make their own decisions at the time and place, and under the circumstances as they see them, consistent with existing policies and procedures. If they do so they should not be second-guessed by someone who was not there at the time. Therefore it is incumbent upon the leader to try to support those decisions whenever possible.

> What a man dislikes in his superiors, let him not display in the treatment of his inferiors.
>
> *Tsang Sin*

Arrogance

Don't be caught up in the power and prestige of your position.

You must always be willing to help subordinates, even with the most mundane tasks. Roll up your sleeves and get your hands dirty when necessary.

Also, remember that you will occasionally make errors. You know that, and your employees know that.

If you have an arrogant attitude, you can expect no help from your subordinates in preventing or correcting your errors.

> To be vain of one's rank or place, is to show that one is below it.
>
> *Leszczynski Stanislaus*

Waste

A major part of your job at any level of your organization is to effectively utilize human and other resources to get the job done.

Wasting any of your resources decreases the efficiency of your unit and is a poor business practice in any industry.

Take the time to plan effectively and ensure that waste is cut to a bare minimum.

> Waste neither time nor money, but make the best use of both.
>
> *Benjamin Franklin*

Conflicts of Interest

Keep in mind that the *perception* of a conflict of interest can be nearly as bad as the real thing.

Avoid preferential treatment in your dealings with suppliers and associates. Don't give it or receive it.

Just as honesty begets honesty, corruption begets corruption.

> There is no odor so bad as that which arises from goodness tainted.
>
> *Henry David Thoreau*

Lying

At all costs.

Never lie to your people or anyone else!

> When a person cannot deceive himself, the chances are against his being able to deceive other people.
>
> *Mark Twain*

Sexual Harassment

In order to avoid sexual harassment, a leader must know and understand exactly what constitutes sexual harassment in the workplace. So pay close attention in the next seminar your company presents on the subject.

Part of your responsibility as a leader is to prevent your subordinates from perpetrating, or being a victim of, sexual harassment.

Ignoring the reality of sexual harassment in the workplace will clearly jeopardize your otherwise successful career.

> Injustice anywhere is a threat to justice everywhere.
>
> *Martin Luther King Jr.*

Loss of Temper

There is little in the world worthy of losing your temper about.

Yet frustrations in the workplace are common and can be difficult to deal with.

As a leader, always try to stay in control. Discuss problems openly with the people involved. Be firm in your demands but remain in control.

Superiors, suppliers, peers, customers, and subordinates will sometimes be infuriating, but losing your temper will probably only compound the problem instead of solving it.

> When angry, count ten before you speak. If very angry, a hundred.
>
> *Thomas Jefferson*

Unsavory Characters

Who are your friends and associates?

Are they the kind of people you should be associating with?
Are they leadership material?

> Associate with men of good quality if you esteem
> your own reputation; for it is better to be alone
> than in bad company.
>
> *George Washington*

Gambling

Whether it's the office sports pool or lottery tickets, gambling
gives the perception of impropriety and a lack of discipline on
your part. Successful people avoid it because they know it is a
loser's game.

> The best throw of the dice is to throw
> them away.
>
> *English Proverb*

Sick Leave

When you are sick, take sick leave. If you are healthy, go to work.

Rest assured that the one day you call in on sick leave to go to the ball game, will be the one time you make the eleven o'clock news as a sports highlight catching a home-run ball.

If you abuse your benefits, your subordinates will also abuse theirs, and you will often be both short-handed and short on respect.

> I would give no thought of what the world might say of me, if I could only transmit to posterity the reputation of an honest man.
>
> *Sam Houston*

Gossip and Rumors

Gossip is idle chatter about the personal affairs of coworkers, generally with a negative connotation. Gossip has no legitimate place in the workplace; discourage it. Rumors spread at work are often based on half-truths or bad information. You may want to investigate negative rumors and find out the truth about them before they undermine your workplace.

In short, avoid gossip and control rumors.

> Silence is the ultimate weapon of power.
>
> *Charles de Gaulle*

Financial Problems

If you can't control your own personal finances, how can you expect your organization to trust you to handle its financial resources effectively?

The same rules that apply to business can also apply to the management of your personal life: planning ahead, conserving resources, and the effective utilization of resources are just a few of these traits.

> He that has a penny in his purse, is worth a penny: Have and you shall be esteemed.
>
> *Petronius*

Blind Loyalty

Loyalty is a leadership trait, but blind loyalty is dangerous.

True loyalty to all involves dedication, support, and sometimes disagreement in an effort to prevent future problems.

However, you cannot support superiors or subordinates who engage in illegal or immoral activities regardless of their motivation.

Avoiding blind loyalty serves the interests of everyone.

> And if the blind lead the blind, both shall fall into the ditch.
>
> *Matthew 15:14*

Alcohol and Drugs

Having too many drinks at the company party has brought down many careers.

Individuals with so little self-control that they fall prey to excessive drinking or drug abuse cannot be expected to have enough self-control to run a department or organization.

> Drunkenness is the failure of a man to control his thoughts.
>
> *David Graysin*

Burnout

The business world is tough.

Burnout can occur in any occupation—in two years or twenty years. To prevent burnout, keep meeting new challenges, either within your organization or in other organizations.

When the work you once found challenging and even fun has turned into drudgery, it is time to move on.

A burned-out leader is no leader at all.

> All looks yellow to a jaundiced eye.
>
> *Alexander Pope*

Illegal Acts

Avoid illegal acts on the job and off the job.

Say no to bribes, kickbacks, and special gifts. Say no to discrimination, labor-law violations, and health and safety code violations.

You must know the law and the consequences of your actions in these areas, or you risk seriously damaging your career.

> A law is valuable not because it is the law, but because there is right in it.
>
> *Henry Ward Beecher*

Emotional Traps

Employees may try to dump personal problems on you.

Go ahead and try to help them, but don't get directly or emotionally involved in their problems or lives.

Remember, as a professional you can listen, recommend, and assist, but you cannot live their lives for them.

Avoid the emotional traps they may set for you.

> The intellect is always fooled by the heart.
>
> *François La Rochefoucauld*

Wow! That's a lot to avoid.

Yes, it is.

The best leaders in industry are a combination of understanding supervisors and competent managers. They also have an understanding of the present and a vision for the future.

You can do everything right—if you work at it.

> The talent of success is nothing more than doing what you can do well, and doing well whatever you do.
>
> *Henry Wadsworth Longfellow*

CHAPTER 19

LEADERS LEAD BY . . .

Here I present the leadership skills that build on all of the skills previously covered. It's a total formula for your success.

> Lead, follow, or get out of the way.
>
> *Thomas Paine*

Assuming the Leadership Role

To be appointed to a leadership position is not sufficient to make you a leader.

You must, after being appointed, take charge and begin leading. Too many people feel that they have *arrived* when they get promoted. The wise know that the promotion is just the beginning.

A leader who assumes the leadership role is much more effective than those who try to succeed by mere position.

It is easier to assume your role once you understand that people want and need to be led by a competent leader. You are there to help them, as well as yourself, by giving them direction.

> When in charge, take charge!
>
> *Unknown*

Thinking in Terms of Solutions

One seldom has to look for problems. They have a natural way of making themselves known.

One does, however, have to look for solutions to those problems.

Rather than expend energy worrying and placing blame, leaders just solve the problem.

Then they go one step further and take action to ensure that a similar problem doesn't occur in the future.

> The block of granite which is an obstacle in the pathway of the weak, becomes a stepping-stone in the pathway of the strong.
>
> *Thomas Carlyle*

Surrounding Themselves with Competence

Leaders are not afraid of subordinates taking their jobs.

Quite the contrary: Leaders recruit the best subordinates they can find. Then they train them thoroughly so they can not only do their job, but so they can also fill in for the leader when necessary.

This ensures that leaders get maximum performance, will be able to take time off, and can be promoted to a higher job, because they have arranged a suitable replacement for their current job.

Quality subordinates are both the result of and the source of strong leadership.

> There is something that is much more scarce, something rarer than ability. It is the ability to recognize ability.
>
> *Robert Half*

Loosely Supervising Subordinates

Leaders ensure that the work is being done, but they allow employees the freedom to do their work in their own way. They encourage employees to make their own decisions and then support those decisions.

They don't stand over employees constantly, checking their every move. Besides, leaders, if they are operating correctly as true leaders, should not have time to oversupervise. Leaders should have too much else to do.

> Trust men and they will be true to you; treat them greatly and they will show themselves great.
>
> *Ralph Waldo Emerson*

Building a Team

Individuals must be treated like part of the team. They must each contribute to the team effort by doing what they do best for the benefit of themselves and the unit.

Leaders put round pegs in round holes, and square pegs in square holes. In this way, those "pegs" are proud of their contribution, they are proud to be a part of the team, and they feel important.

Leaders should think and speak in terms of "we" and "ours," and they should encourage their subordinates to do the same.

It's all about a team effort to get the job done.

> The man who gets the most satisfactory results is not always the man with the most brilliant single mind, but rather the man who can best coordinate the brains and talents of his associates.
>
> *W. Alton Jones*

Respecting Subordinates

Leaders find time to listen to their subordinates.

The ability to be creative, to have vision, and to be an informed professional is not limited to management personnel alone. Subordinates often have valuable ideas for improving products and services.

True leaders treat each person as a unique individual. They recognize strengths and weaknesses, and accept both.

> Men are respectable only as they respect.
>
> *Ralph Waldo Emerson*

Encouraging Subordinates

People want to learn and grow. They also want the opportunity to advance.

Leaders show employees where they can go in the organization and help them to get there.

They give of themselves, their time, their knowledge, and their experience in order to ensure that their subordinates can grow. They arrange for employees to have opportunities for training and advancement.

They don't worry about people leaving their unit because they have their employees' long-term welfare in mind.

What better position could they be in than to get promoted and find several of their former employees in that new unit—employees that they encouraged and assisted to be all that they could be? The result of a leader's past support will be loyalty that cannot be obtained any other way.

> It is . . . management's job to enable the enterprise and each of its members to grow and develop.
>
> *Peter Drucker*

Teaching Effectively

Perhaps no other area of leadership can have such long-lasting and rewarding results.

We can all remember those whom we worked for who took us under their wings and showed us the ropes.

As a leader, it is you who are now obligated to do the same for your subordinates.

When the people you teach reach higher positions in the organization, you will feel the rewards of a teacher.

In the interim, your teaching efforts will make your employees better workers, which will benefit you, your unit, and the organization.

> A teacher affects eternity; he can never tell where his influence stops.
>
> *Henry Adams*

Handling Ambiguity Well

Life is so simple at the bottom. The boss gives you a specific job to do and you do it.

As you move up the hierarchy, the work becomes less defined. The boss gives you a mandate to solve a problem and gives you little else. It is up to you to define the parameters of the task, figure out how to finance it, and find the time to get it done.

Leaders thrive on this kind of work. Ambiguity is a type of freedom for them to be creative and innovative. It challenges them and allows them to turn their own thoughts into actions.

The initial lack of direction would bother many employees but not a true leader.

> I believe that the true road to preeminent success in any line, is to make yourself master of that line.
>
> *Andrew Carnegie*

Taking Risks

Leaders take *calculated* risks!

Leaders are not foolhardy, wild-eyed maniacs who throw away the rule book.

On the contrary, leaders continually evaluate the elements of a risky project in comparison to the potential for gain from taking those risks.

They speak out in the heat of controversy. They take a stand for what is right but not necessarily popular. They dare to try new ideas, sure in their own minds that their ideas will work.

They do not risk the safety of their subordinates or someone else's career—only their own.

> It is impossible to win the great prizes of life without running risks.
>
> *Theodore Roosevelt*

Striving to Be the Best

In everything they do.

Leaders also instill this attribute in their subordinates.

Leaders work hard and seek to be the best—for their own satisfaction.

> Get a good idea and stay with it. Dog it, and work at it until it's done and done right.
>
> *Walt Disney*

Taking Responsibility

True leaders are in charge, and they are responsible for every facet of the project.

When it is successful, they are the ones responsible. When it is unsuccessful, they are also the ones responsible.

Taking responsibility relieves others and shows them who the true leader really is.

> A chief is a man who assumes responsibility. He says, "I was beaten." He does not say, "My men were beaten." Thus speaks a real man.
>
> *Antoine de Saint-Exupéry*

Running Ahead of the Pack

Leaders are a little more progressive than their subordinates.

- They are a little more innovative.
- They are a little more creative.
- They take that extra step.
- They spend a little more effort.
- They get a little more accomplished.
- They get a few more results.
- They get promoted a little sooner.

However, they can also run a little too far ahead of the pack. They need support from others to be successful. If they're too far ahead, others can't keep up. If others can't keep up, they can't help their leaders if they encounter trouble.

So, unless you want to go it completely alone, keep ahead—but not too far ahead.

> It is a mistake to look too far ahead. Only one link in the chain of destiny can be handled at a time.
>
> *Winston Churchill*

Always Going Forward

Leaders are always going forward, sometimes in tiny steps, but usually in quantum leaps.

A leader's group is the first to try new technologies, and first in efficiency and productivity.

The group doesn't increase its productivity by hundredths of a percent; it increases productivity by full percentage points. It can even double or triple past performances.

True leaders make things happen in a big way.

> Even if you're on the right track, you'll get run over if you just sit there.
>
> *Arthur Godfrey*

Example

One Fortune 500 executive told his people, "You may do anything you see me doing."

Subordinates will emulate, consciously or subconsciously, their bosses.

If you are forward thinking, innovative, and progressive, then your department will move consistently forward.

True leaders are also willing to roll up their shirtsleeves and do whatever is necessary to make a project succeed. Their commitment and dedication in such a situation sets the example for all of their people.

True leaders are excellent role models.

> The example of good men is visible philosophy.
> *English Proverb*

Having Vision

To be able to visualize the completed project, the final goal, and all of its rewards and consequences is the ultimate test for true leaders.

In addition to visualizing "the dream," they must also be able to visualize each task that must be completed, and the integration of those tasks, to successfully complete the project.

Such vision is dependent upon all of the attributes, actions, and efforts described in previous sections of this book. To true leaders, vision defines the final goal, and action is the path that leads to the vision.

> We have always held to the hope, the belief,
> the conviction that there is a better life, a better
> world, beyond the horizon.
>
> *Franklin D. Roosevelt*

Exhibiting Good Common Sense

Well, we are now back to the title and essence of this little book: *Common Sense Management*.

Is common sense inborn? Maybe.

The result of experience? Maybe.

The combination of intelligence, knowledge, and experience? Probably!

The experts can argue what constitutes common sense until the end of time.

However, the fact remains that a true leader has it. Period!

> Common sense is the knack of seeing things as they are, and doing things as they ought to be done.
>
> *Josh Billings*

CHAPTER 20

QUICK WISDOM: LEADERSHIP

Once appointed to a leadership position, you can be a positive influence on your people and the organization, or you can represent everything that is wrong in the promotional process.

Here are some real-world guidelines to help you know where you are on the scale of success and failure.

25 Positive Traits That Can Help Potential Leaders

1. Sociability
2. Trustworthiness
3. Warmth
4. Supportiveness
5. Independence
6. Dependability
7. Leadership incentive
8. Competitive nature
9. Assertiveness
10. Ability to listen
11. Fairness
12. Loyalty
13. Flexibility
14. Reliability
15. Generosity
16. Dynamic personality
17. Adaptability
18. Tough-mindedness
19. Versatility
20. Cooperation
21. Risk taking
22. Approachability
23. Ability to cope
24. Orientation to people
25. Responsibility

25 Negative Traits That Can Hinder Potential Leaders

1. Lack of knowledge
2. Disinterest in work
3. Negative attitude
4. Constant complaining
5. Lack of social skills
6. Self-centered demeanor
7. Inability to speak in public
8. Arrogance
9. Interruption of others
10. Poor appearance
11. Indecision
12. Failure to listen
13. Poor posture
14. Tendency to talk too much
15. Insecurity
16. Impatience
17. Irresponsibility
18. Lack of enthusiasm
19. Lack of dependability
20. Argumentativeness
21. Poor personal hygiene
22. Preoccupation
23. Lack of personal integrity
24. Overreaction
25. Lack of concern for others

> In order to be a leader a man must have followers. And to have followers, a man must have their confidence. Hence, the supreme quality for a leader is unquestionably integrity. Without it, no real success is possible, whether it is on a section gang, a football field, in an army, or in an office.
>
> *Dwight D. Eisenhower*

EPILOGUE: MAKING IT ALL HAPPEN

You now know the basics of how to be a successful supervisor, manager, and leader in your industry. The rest is up to you.

But here is what our panel of experts says about the possibilities for your career:

> Success in business requires training and discipline and hard work. But if you're not frightened by these things, the opportunities are just as great today as they ever were.
>
> *David Rockefeller*

> Always bear in mind that your own resolution to succeed is more important than any one thing.
>
> *Abraham Lincoln*

And, finally, from humorist Will Rogers:

> Common sense ain't common.

Along with these thinkers, I sincerely hope that this book, and its words of advice and wisdom of the ages, help you to develop a successful career in your chosen profession.

My best wishes to you, the people you work with, and the family you support through your success in the workplace.